From Heart and Mind:
A Classroom Odyssey

Stanley J. Bezuszka

Dale Seymour Publications

To my sister, Josephine Bezuszka Kokoska, who has made possible the opportunity for my many years of teaching.

Editor: Joan D. Martin
Editorial Consultant: Margaret J. Kenney
Project Editor: Joan Gideon
Cover Design: Rachel Gage
Production Coordinator: Claire Flaherty

Order number DS33210
ISBN 0-86651-756-1

1 2 3 4 5 6 7 8 9 10-DR-96 95 94 93 92

DALE
SEYMOUR
PUBLICATIONS
P.O. BOX 10888
PALO ALTO, CA 94303

Made from
Recycled Paper

Contents

About the Author

Stanley J. Bezuszka, S.J., a native of Poland, arrived in the USA at an early age and received his primary and secondary education in Lowell, Massachusetts. After entering the Jesuit order he continued his academic pursuits at Weston College, Boston College, and Brown University. Father Bezuszka has had a long and distinguished career in mathematics education. He has led well over 900 presentations, workshops, and minicourses of a mathematical nature in this country and overseas. These presentations have been marked with deep insights about mathematics content and the teaching and learning of mathematics. His talks and conversation are invariably punctuated with humorous stories and anecdotes, the majority of which pertain to teachers, students, and their environment. His years of experience as a mathematics teacher at the university level and as a frequent visitor to classrooms that run the gamut K–12, have provided a wealth of subject matter for his lively imagination and keen mind to capture in print. This collection of reflective, motivational, and perceptive excerpts from his presentations, although targeted especially for those who teach mathematics, will in large part have special meaning for all who have a commitment to education.

In 1990 the National Council of Supervisors of Mathematics honored their colleague in mathematics education and presented Stanley Bezuszka, S.J. with the Glenn Gilbert Award for his outstanding service to the profession.

Preface

Odyssey:

- Any series of wanderings especially when filled with notable experiences.
- A long adventurous journey.
- A spiritual or intellectual quest

" . . . and gladly would he learn and gladly teach . . . "

G. Chaucer,
The Canterbury Tales

Over the past many years I have been privileged to address teachers of mathematics. For these opportunities I am sincerely grateful. Over these same years, from casual conversations with those who were in my audience and from others by correspondence, I have learned that the mathematical content of my talks though appreciated was often a distant second to the motivational elements that I frequently interjected and developed. I have often felt the same myself listening to many excellent speakers at NCTM conferences and at meetings of various mathematics groups. I enjoyed and learned a great deal from their mathematics content but I recalled their motivational message time and again to help me through critical moments in the classroom. Such inspirational recalls are necessary for our blue Mondays and frantic Fridays.

Now as the shadows grow longer from the setting sun of my days, days whose past number far outnumber the days of my future, I have with some reluctance agreed to put together a few of the thoughts on motivation which have been my own source of inspiration as a teacher. Hopefully, they will serve the same purpose for my teacher friends, both present and future.

A word about the ideas and materials presented here. Many of the ideas are my own. Most of the classroom incidences happened to me personally. However, over the years I have also heard many things which I have adapted, assimilated, and transformed. I have seen some incidences which have been embellished almost beyond recognition. I regret that because of my rather frail memory, I am unable to acknowledge fully and gratefully by name those to whom I have listened or whose works I have read or in whose company I have experienced such happy and often hilarious episodes. I do wish to thank most sincerely all those friends whose contributions have made my life richer and my classroom experiences more enjoyable.

This text is not to be read like a novel at one sitting. It is to be kept on the desk, sampled, reflected upon, and savored.

My life has been interwoven with those of teachers. They have been years of love for their friendship and especially years of admiration for their unselfish giving of themselves for students. These are men and women who sacrifice themselves each day where only the One who called them to teach, daily witnesses their love and service for His "Little Ones."

This booklet is a tribute to the many teachers who teach the material of their classes not only from the mind but also from the heart.

S. J. B., S.J.

Chapter 1
The Tradition of Mathematics

Many of you no doubt remember the introduction to the *Fiddler on the Roof*. The interlocutor asks the protagonist Tevye, how he and his people have managed to survive all those years of ever present persecution, the years of forced wanderings in the countries of the world, the days and the nights of cold, of hunger, of beating poverty. They had suffered rejection by their neighbors; were under constant harassment by their enemies; were often rejected by their friends; and were rejected time and again even by their God. In answer to the question of what is the powerful source of his peoples' survival, Tevye simply raises his hand and says one word:

TRADITION

Tradition is an important inheritance of all races, all cultures, all beliefs. Tradition and the content of tradition is the foundation of society, of education, and the most important unit of all society, the human family.

Mathematicians are a special family of teachers, of researchers, of developers of mathematics. Mathematicians are prime movers of our society—and our family has a tradition and a glorious heritage.

What is the content and spirit of tradition?

Tradition is an inherited culture, but more, it is an inherited spirit, it is an attitude to a culture. And so, the tradition of mathematics is a culture and a spirit of mathematics, a content, and an attitude to mathematics.

Mathematics began, rather it was born, on the day that our ancestors gazed fascinated and thrilled at the physical universe that was their home. Mathematics was born in the wonder of the human spirit.

1

This mathematics was transmitted in the magical weave of words and symbols—and so it has continued through the many generations of unrecorded events, where slowly or rapidly, answers accumulated to the questions of our ancestors and solutions were found for some of their wonderings.

And so the heritage, the tradition, the story of mathematics is a history of the pilgrimage of the human mind seeking to understand the mysteries of the universe and to find answers to the many wonders and many questions of men and women.

This colorful and dramatic quest has been carried on by equally human and forceful men and women, whose vision went beyond all visible boundaries—men and women who possessed intuition, insight, a poet's imagination, and perhaps even a touch of irrational obsession. The math makers and teachers are an important part of our civilization. They have left us a lasting heritage of the mind. This heritage is a colorful and dramatic quest for the practical and the apparently useless, an enigmatic mixture of reality and dreams.

And so there is this dual aspect of the heritage of mathematics:

- there is the practical, the applicable, the economically indispensable, and
- the fanciful, the imaginative, the inspired insight of the creative aspirations of the human mind.

Both aspects have always been characteristic of mathematics.

You know, the sun could set in a mist or a fog. The result would be the same. But instead, it often sets in a blaze of glory and flaming color. People's hearts sing and they are happy.

Why does it happen this way? I don't know.

But it is there, the impractical, the beautiful, the great splendor, designed not for the human head but for the human heart.

And it is the same with our splendid tradition and heritage of mathematics—often designed and meant for the human mind, but also with a mystical charm, giving joy to the human heart.

The great mathematicians are our ancestors whose creativity has enriched our lives—this creativity that is a mysterious talent that explodes like the 4th of July rockets and colorfully lights up the intellectual lives of people of all nations.

What is this remarkable talent of creativity, this creativity

- that sees what is hidden and invisible to others,
- that extends the frontiers of human thought that are barriers to the thinking of other humans?

Creativity is born of insatiable curiosity and nurtured by imagination.

Creativity is a talent neither enhanced by a wealth of accessible resources nor frustrated by the lack of available opportunities.

Creativity when possessed is a driving force that is heedless of human solicitous cautions for health or wealth, and ignores both social acclaim as well as social ostracism.

Creativity is perhaps imitable by supreme personal effort, but oh, how glorious when it is just a gift bestowed.

And so today and every day, we need this special spirit of creativity and especially new ideas for the music in ourselves, ideas to live and work by—great swinging ideas to which our dreams march.

We need leaders, tall men and women, sun-crowned people who live above the fog in their thinking. We teachers need occasions that will help us, will give us courage, ideas, and inspiration. One of those thrilling moments, small enough to pack away and keep forever, yet large enough to lean against when we get weary and discouraged.

And so as mortals, with emotions and feelings, we find that our teaching has moments of discouragement, frustration, and futility.

We teachers need to ensure that we perpetuate ourselves by encouraging the young to enter our profession.

Without teachers,
- all people are just plain people,uninspired and uninspiring,

Without teachers,
- there are only people unaware of how far they can go or what they can achieve,

Without teachers, people are just ordinary people.

Without teachers,
- there are no heroes
- there are no scholars,
- there are no saints,
- there are no great scientists,
- there are no outstanding humanists,
- there are just nobodies.

Without teachers,
- there are men and women, human beings without the divine spark of humanity, without wings to chase the sun, without dreams to be free of this earth, without hope of being raised to just one step below the angels.

With teachers,
- nobodies become somebodies,
- students become scholars, saints, and heroes.

With teachers,
- dreams in young hearts are ever renewed and fulfilled,
- these are hearts that will ever be grateful because of you,
- there is a glorious heritage to be preserved for the future.

For to be a teacher is to be a fellow traveler in the caravan of the Magi—to have as a goal, a destiny guided by a Star.

There is an old Hebrew saying:
> Two things a man must do for himself, with which even God cannot help him
> To make a friend and to find a teacher.

And often in the classroom, many discover that the teacher and the friend are one and the same person.

∼ *Interlude* ∼
Take It on Faith

The following is a logical response from a highly respected mathematician.

The mathematician and I were attending a meeting along with Max Beberman. In the evening, we were enjoying a social hour together. Max turned to the mathematician and said, "I hear that you're an atheist."

The mathematician readily admitted to this. Max folded his arms, beamed and looking at me said, "Well Stan, take it from here."

I could think of no clever comeback, so I weakly countered with, "How do you know that there is no God?"

The mathematician looked at me and said, "You know, Father, there are some things you just have to take on faith."

During the height of the "publish or perish" era, the president of Boston College, a Jesuit, was bent on establishing this policy. Somehow he found out that I did not share his enthusiasm for "publish or perish." He warned me if I did not subscribe to his "publish or perish" policy, that for me, it would be "publish or parish."

Chapter 2
Origins and Symbol Weavers

The Symbol Weavers

The Symbol Weavers over centuries, the mathematicians, have left us a heritage and a tradition. This dual legacy, heritage and tradition, has inspired many young men and women not only to make mathematics a career, but also to become teachers of mathematics and to carry on the tradition of the great mathematicians.

Mathematics is often compared to music because of its symbolism. The comparison is valid and striking. Just as a symphony conductor can hear internal music from the little dots and swirls of the music score, so also the mathematician reads the score for the symphony of the universe in the symbols of mathematics.

Arturo Toscanini studied the score of the new symphony intently. He then sat back in his chair and closed his eyes. Suddenly the room began to fill with music. Toscanini slowly raised his hands. The invisible orchestra responded to the gentle swaying of his hands. Soft violins sang and sweet flutes responded. Horns broke in and were silenced by the crashing drums.

The world's great conductors of symphony orchestras can transform the small dots on lined paper into real inner music.

The score for the symphony of the universe is written in the symbols of mathematics. Like the musician's notes, the mathematician's formulas capture the music of the whirling planets and the song of the singing spheres. The sun rises on cue, the stars move majestically in space. Lightning crashes and waves break thundering to shore.

All this the mathematician sees and hears in the swirl of a letter, the curve of a symbol, or the slant of a line.

The world is filled with silent symphonies captured by the magic of the symbol weavers. The mind can read and fill our hearts with song!

And so forever, the world will be filled with the silent symphonies captured by the magic of the Symbol Weavers.

$\approx$

The great mathematicians wrote mathematics that whispers immortality with each symbol and each word. And so when they die one is not convinced that they are really dead.

$\approx$

And what are some of these permanent attributes of mathematics that have been fostered and transmitted in the glorious history of mathematics?

Let us recall a little of the history of our mathematics heritage. Mathematics, in its earliest origins, was conceived by the mind of man struggling for daily survival—but it was nurtured by the profitless dreams of the mind of man, in the challenge to count the grains of sand on the seashore, or number the limitless stars in the heavens.

$\approx$

The One, the Many, and the All

The history of mankind is a story of a never ending quest. The eternal search began with man's starry eyed wonder at the world he saw for the first time. What? And how? And most of all: Why? We would live and toil to understand. The heritage of knowledge would be transmitted to new generations, but not the consuming urge for wisdom. This was a gift born in humans.

The past centuries record changing theories about our world. Yet in all the diversity appears the unshaken conviction that there is an underlying unity and simplicity in nature. There must be a basic ONE to explain the mysterious MANY.

Philosophers, scientists, and mathematicians have proposed ONES to account for all change. The ONE must explain the infinite variety of forms, shapes, and colors. It must explain the infinitesimally small and unbelievably large. It must reveal the pattern of unity in the world and make the mysterious universe intelligible.

Today, we have added a modern ONE to the host of ONES given by ancients. From a tradition begun in the scientific era of Galileo and developed in the eighteenth and nineteenth centuries was born a new conviction.

It was adopted by the twentieth century. It will influence the future centuries.

ALL IS MATHEMATICS!

Even though we do not know the exact answers to the many questions on the origins of mathematics, we can search the records and make a few reasonable deductions. Such a historical reconstruction possesses certain advantages. In spite of the impressive record of past and present mathematicians, mathematics is still a wide open subject whose frontiers are ever expanding. Perhaps there is still someone with a fresh viewpoint, a different interpretation that will open new and challenge the old fields of thought. This can be done only by re-examining the roots of the subject.

Dreams and Bread

> Look on my works,
> ye Mighty, and despair!

The Pharaoh looked and was pleased. For twenty years, one hundred thousand men had sweated and strained to make his dream come true. Now the task was finished. The Great Pyramid of Cheops was a wonder to behold. It was to be the first of the ancient world's great wonders.

But Egypt was not just a visionary's kingdom. This land of dreams was also a land of bread. The rich soil from the overflowing Nile yielded a golden harvest of wheat so plentiful that Egypt became known as the granary of the world. The many ships in the harbors of Thebes and Memphis brought men from distant shores who spoke in strange accents. They returned home to tell the marvels of this new land in words that awed and amazed their listeners. Traders leading long caravans from the East bartered the products of their nation's skilled hands for Egypt's life-sustaining grain. They lingered at Alexandria and left reluctantly. On the long journey back to their own lands they made plans to return to Egypt and to wander no more. Such was the magic spell cast by Egypt.

The story of Egypt, with minor variations is the story of mankind. For past centuries humans have been a puzzling mixture of the practical and the ideal.

For all the uncounted years of the future, our goal will always extend beyond our grasp. We in the present are the echo of yesterday and the prophecy of tomorrow. From the wisdom and accomplishments of the past we see that very little worthwhile is achieved without dreams.

> We have two sides to our head:
> One for dreams and one for bread.

~

> My sleepless head spins dreams—
> While their tireless hands knead bread!

> And so we spend our days and nights—
> Both are needed in this world
> The dreams and the bread!

~

Math Makers

Leonardo da Vinci, the great artist, scientist, and engineer, was born in 1452. His notebooks contained sketches and calculations for underwater boats. He dreamed of man flying in space with the freedom of the eagle. It took almost five hundred years before da Vinci's ideas were turned into submarines to explore the ocean and airplanes to navigate the skies.

Isaac Newton was born in 1642. His mathematics contained the explanation of the motion of the planets. It took us three hundred years to use Newton's ideas and send up earth satellites and put men into space.

George Boole was born in 1815. In his mathematical papers he wrote about binary operators and the wonders of logic. It took us more than one hundred years to convert Boole's mathematics into the enormous high speed computers of today.

Emmy Noether was born in 1882. After her death in 1935, Albert Einstein remarked that Emmy's enormous contributions to algebra would benefit future generations of mathematicians.

In the past, the pure mathematician has been far ahead of the applied mathematician and engineer—has dreamed of wonderful worlds that would never be seen personally.

The pure mathematician is most happy when he or she is most general, most abstract. The pure mathematician develops mathematical theories, and is interested in knowledge for its own sake. The applied mathematician puts knowledge to practical use in the production of our ever-increasing material needs. Today, the pure mathematician and the applied mathematician work together. They continually exchange ideas and problems. The person whose head is in the clouds works with the person whose feet are solidly planted on the ground.

The world today needs both the pure mathematician and the applied mathematician. It needs both the dreamer and the person who can turn the dreams into steel and mortar.

The glorious future planned in the mind of the pure mathematician becomes the marvelous present in the hands of the brilliant applied mathematician.

Truth cannot be invented.
It must be discovered!

∽

Mathematician's Imagination

To work and strive and finally to possess that mathematician's imagination that transcends time and space, the dream of wanting to see and know what no one else has seen or known before—this imagination whose enduring charm is nourished by curiosity and perpetual wonder.

Beyond the Stars

To travel beyond the stars! A dream of all which translated simply means
- to walk where no one has walked before,
- to create what has not been created before,
- to be a flame forever for the dark nights of the minds of all.

The Old, the Wise and Dreams

They tell me that only in the very old and the very wise that you do not see dreams in their eyes.
But our students are young and free, instead of old and wise.
The lives of the young are such stuff as "dreams are made of."
There is time enough when old and wise they'll be
And so now dreams are for them, visions that teachers can inspire.

Never let another eagle determine how high you yourself will fly.

"Those who do not put faith in dreams have left only to clutch at shadows and chase the wind."
adaptation of Eccles.5:6

Search for Truth

It is reported that Mark Kac, an outstanding Polish mathematician and scientist of this century, once commented about his chosen career:

"In search for truth, I left my people, my country, and my family. It should not therefore be assumed that I shall forsake truth for any lesser motive."

And so we continue the slow but passionate search for order. And not in vain. For order is the everlasting stronghold of reason.

Life Is Not Logic

Students take geometry presumably to learn reasoning and logic. It is only after many years of living that they discover that life is not logic, that it is not a series of "If . . . thens" or "If and only ifs." If geometry was taught instead as an art, then geometry would expand and enrich the lives of students in school and certainly after they have left school.

I have found in my reading over the years that the great mathematicians in their speeches and writings were not emphasizing the logical aspects of mathematics. Instead, they kept repeating that imagination, insight, and creative intuition were the keynote elements in mathematics.

But more important for mathematics than logic is imagination and the wonderful freedom to create and to invent, and the pleasure of finding some relation which previously one did not see or suspect.

Dreams and Nightmares
The dream of deriving all of mathematics from logic has turned out to be a nightmare for some mathematicians.

~

Beyond the Edge of Space
The mystery of space has terrified and fascinated the earthbound!

For centuries, our earth was considered a flatland. Humans were prisoners on earth guarded by horrible creatures in the darkness of the surrounding space. Explorers and adventurers were cautioned not to venture beyond known frontiers, for beyond the boundaries of the earth there was only the fearsome void, a grave for foolhardy trespassers.

Ferdinand Magellan challenged the convictions of his day. He sailed the seas beyond the human fears of man. Earth was a prison, but one which could be safely circled forever. Magellan solved the riddle of the earth but not the mystery of space.

Today, astronauts have made a home in the sky. They have walked unpaved streets and uncharted paths in space. Humans have surpassed the eagle in flight and have shattered the bonds of earth.

And yet, space is only a symbol. It stands for the unknown, a cell that confines the mind more effectively than steel and concrete. Our knowledge of space urges us onward. The conquest of space is a victory for our spirit!

> No rest does the weary climber seek
> If he finds but one unconquered peak!

~

Unsolved Puzzles
There are so many puzzles in our world, that even if it were to exist for all eternity, it is quite possible that not all of them would be solved or answered.

~

Enchantment of Numbers

Let me comment briefly on the enchantment of numbers. Numbers have always fascinated us. The early history of mathematics is practically a history of numbers. Theologians, philosophers, scientists, and professional and recreational mathematicians have all contributed to the development of number theory and the lore of numbers.

But a great deal of nonsense has also been written about numbers, which does not detract from the fact that there have been some significant discoveries about the nature, properties, and relations among numbers.

Eternal mathematics is not created out of the necessities of the present day. It develops in leisure away from the pressures and needs of society.

The gift of numbers like the gift of fire has made the world much brighter.

The transforming power of the mathematics of the master is a true paradox. With insight and imagination, a content has been created that is forever young with new applications and yet whose roots are as old as mankind.

Mathematics as an Onion and a Pomegranate

Some people treat mathematics like an onion—they go on peeling layer after layer hoping to find out what mathematics is all about and at the end they only have nothing.

Mathematics is like a pomegranate—there are delightful tidbits everywhere. You break it and at first nothing is visible and then you remove a thin layer of skin and there are the seeds—a delightful surprise and a pleasure.

How I Feel about Mathematics

Math is a many splendored thing—
For those who hold in awe the gift of mind—
Who prize even more dearly the grace of insight.

Math is a many splendored thing—
For those who fuse mind and insight,
By the alchemy of inspiration into creative kinship—
With Him who once proclaimed:
"Let there be light."

~

Thrill of Discovery

Every generation of students makes its own discoveries—discoveries of things already discovered and in some instances, new discoveries.

The thrill of a new discovery is assuredly much greater than the thrill of rediscovery—but both produce a thrill that makes mathematics enjoyable and exciting.

~

The finished product in mathematics shows the inspiration not the perspiration.

~

The Timely and the Timeless

"Give me a place to stand and I will move the Earth."
Archimedes

The only sound in the room was the monotonous tick-tock, tick-tock of the clock. A young man sat quietly, listening intently. Then, reaching for a pencil, he wrote a few symbols on the paper at his desk. That night Albert Einstein (1879–1955) stated the mystery of time in an equation. Relativity was a summary of the past and the secret of the future.

Time haunts us from our first heartbeat. One must invent the timely to survive and to progress. The wheel changed a plodding people into a mobile society. The steam engine welded our frontiers into a nation. Electricity moved the country dweller into the turmoil of industrial cities. The power of the shattered atom will in all probability break the bonds that confine us to this planet earth.

Yet in spite of all this striving for the timely, we are forever attempting to write, to paint, to create, to discover the timeless. The timely, when introduced into a society, changes the mode of doing things. The timeless can change the pattern of the world's thinking.

Mathematics has in it the timely and the timeless, and yet it is not isolated from the realities of each day. But creative and imaginative minds are needed to produce the effective surprises hidden in its lasting principles. The Earth movers will always be the young men and women who combine the timely with the timeless.

We have structured mathematics logically. Now let's structure it psychologically.

Mathematicians Share Qualities

Mathematics for many has been a pure science dealing only with computation and measurement. These are the commonplace, mundane, and tedious aspects of mathematics that are boring even to mathematicians. Very seldom do these people come into contact with any elements of mathematics which are not exclusively concerned with numbers and computation. Thus, for them mathematics is a dry and cold subject unsuited for the development of imagination, insight and creativity.

However, logic and reasoning, though they are indispensable for some aspects of mathematics, are not the exclusive characteristics and properties of mathematics. Insight, imagination, fantasy and the miracle of intuition constitute the essence and soul of the creative mathematician. And so mathematicians often share the same qualities possessed by poets, musicians, painters, architects and philosophers.

We must present the history of mathematics with care and discernment. What discourages many of our mathematics students is the overwhelming description of versatility in the giants of mathematics so that what was intended to be inspiration ends with student desperation.

~

The great mathematicians were obsessed with creative ideas. They had the insight, the intuition and most of all the tenacity to pursue these ideas to completion. This is why they have left us a rich and noble heritage.

~

"Mathematics studies non-existing things and is able to find out the full truth about them."
Socrates

~

The Hindu System of Numeration

No one knows the real origin of the legend. But the story has been passed on from generation to generation. Teachers still tell it, parents recall it, and children enjoy it.

One day Raman, the great Hindu teacher was resting in the shade of a margosa tree. He nodded and daydreamed a little for his past years had been busy with much work and many travels. He recalled the magic land of the Egyptians, the ever-fresh beauty of the Tigris-Euphrates Valley. He remembered the delicate writings of the Nile people and the strange sharp imprints of the Babylonians.

Wouldn't it be wonderful if he could capture the charm and the power of the writing of these distant peoples for his own young students? Raman's eyes grew heavy and he slept. In his dream he saw strange symbols written in the sand. Raman awoke and copied as well as he could remember:

1 2 3 3 8 9 6 ∧ 8 9

But one symbol was missing. What was it? The sun broke through the branches of the tree and Raman looked up. Suddenly he remembered. The missing symbol was the round fullness of the life-sustaining sun:

And so the Hindu numerals were born in a fanciful myth destined to become the first great tale from India.

Simon Stevin, a Belgian, belongs with the legend of India. In the last half of the sixteenth century he broke away from cumbersome fractions and introduced decimals, but his complicated notation hindered the general acceptance of his brilliant idea. Perhaps, unlike Raman, no vision enlightened Stevin. Yet once more the East inspired the West and others found a solution. Perhaps the ○ of Raman was made smaller and filled in until it became . . . our decimal point!

Mathematics: A Language, a Science, an Art

Mathematics was and is man and woman conceived, man and woman developed. Mathematics was created by the first person drawing crude marks on the wall of a cave to tally possessions. Mathematics was created by the merchants in the market place who bartered treasures from the remote corners of the earth for the necessities of life. Mathematics was created by the solitary men and women who speculated about the proportions of figures and the motions of the heavenly bodies.

Mathematics today is created by the men and women in universities and technological research centers who challenge the existing boundaries of time and space. Mathematics is created by the person in the street by every relation he or she discovers to generalize a portion of their experience.

Mathematics was and will continue to be a language, a science and an art.

Mathematics is a language.

Mathematics, a system of definite concepts specialized in content and form, is distinctive in its communication patterns of technical words and refined symbolism. But mathematics is more than the study of symbols or the acquisition of proficiency and skill in their manipulation. Behind the marks and conventional signs there is the domain of concepts and ideas clearly defined and sensitively expressed. The abstract is for the moment caught in the slant of a line or the shape of a letter. Men and women work with the lines and figures and characters—and relations previously vaguely suspected or indistinctly perceived now appear confirmed and clear and ordered. Mathematics conveys ideas in a language of signs and symbols whose eloquence has charmed people in all ages.

Mathematics is a science.

Mathematics has the elements of a science—a systematized body of knowledge, organized and ordered with a unity and beauty of a living organism which while ever changing, growing, and developing can still be recognized in each age for itself.

Mathematics is an art.

Mathematics is an art that experiments with new concepts, redesigns the old, constructs and fashions ideas with skill and taste, proportion and rigor, simplicity and grace. As an art, mathematics requires the same perfection and talent that elevates and proclaims the masters in every field in each century: the Homers, the Shakespeares, the Brontes, the Beethovens, and the Leonardo da Vincis.

Every person in every age shares in and adds to the heritage of mathematics that will forever remain a tribute to the voice, the mind, and the spirit of man.

The mathematician's imagination is nourished by curiosity and perpetual wonder.

Mathematics will make a significant contribution to the understanding of some of the problems in this world as long as human curiosity and imagination endure.

The Glory of Mathematics

Any lyric exaggeration of the charm and power of mathematics must always be tempered by sane moderation and reasoned judgment.

Mathematics cannot touch you with even the slightest spark of love, for it has no heart.

It cannot teach you sympathy, for it has no feeling.

It cannot make you glad, for its voice is mute and the worship in the temple of logic is to an idol with big ugly human feet.

Mathematics is the product of the human mind and neither its origin nor its results are stamped with divinity.

But like a scaffolding that is useful for a time and a purpose and then is torn down and burnt, so mathematics will be studied, learned, and taught until time ends and men and women have no more need of props and stays.

Some traditions should be allowed to remain and grow—but best of all are the traditions that should be and are imitated.

Continuity of Tradition

The continuity of mathematical tradition depends on students and teachers. And in the history of the tradition of mathematics, the crowning achievement in any age is the new mathematics major or mathematics teacher.

Our Link

The heritage of mathematics is our link with the past and our legacy for the future.

∾ *Interlude* ∾
Experience vs. Youth

At a youthful age it seems that intelligence is more important than experience. In the twilight years it seems that experience is more important than intelligence.

In some things that depend upon experience, we teachers, are smarter than our students. But in those instances that require common sense, we teachers have no right or claim to superiority.

No amount of schooling can take the place of brains and common sense. Brains and common sense have made many persons successful who have had very little schooling.

Experience, that wonderful knowledge, intuition, and insight that enables you to recognize a mistake when you've made it again and again and again. . . .

Chapter 3
Teacher's Goals

A Teacher's Goals
The teaching goal of teachers is ever to advance:
- to advance beyond present frontiers,
- to advance beyond the boundaries set by the stars.

The goal of a teacher is to know no boundaries.

If my heart believes it, my mind can achieve it.

What is the task of a teacher? To help a child discover a truly great love—your love.

A Teacher's Obligation
It is the obligation of the teacher, demanding all and full effort to show:
- that a mind trained for imaginative thinking is more important than a mind trained only for the gathering of facts
- that the important thing is not so much that every child should be taught, as that every child should be given the desire to learn
- that learning can and should be a glorious and enjoyable personal adventure lasting a lifetime.

And only teachers can give this kind of inspiration. Only teachers can give this kind of leadership.

You don't become a teacher and love teaching for a minute, a day, or for a year. You must love it forever.

A Teacher's Fulfillment
The fulfillment of a teacher is to have students
- master the subject so well as to be not only a critic but also a rival,
- eventually learn and know more about the subject taught than the teacher does.

Cynic: I can make a better world than the present one.
Sage: Go to it. That's why God created you.

A teacher's task is to destroy the obstacles that students place in their own education.

I taught mathematics like the skiing instructor who endlessly drilled students at the base of the mountain.

Occasionally and only when all the exercises had been completed would I let them take on the mountain's challenge. Then I was surprised to discover that it was not my drills but the spirit and challenge of the mountain that called them to perfect and enjoy their skills.

We are teachers opening the doors to tomorrow each day.

My Best

What motivates me to give my best in each class? As I end each class, I put down the chalk and pick up the eraser—my class leaves and neither of us knows if we will meet again.

～

Dreams in Their Eyes

Not even the very old or the very wise,
Can live without dreams in their eyes.

～

A teacher must always remember that for the young there are no dreams too big, no innovations which are unimaginable, and no frontiers beyond their reach.

～

"If you never have a dream, you'll never have a dream come true", so sang a nation and then proved it true. The same is true about mathematics—dream and it will come true.

～

The world will live tomorrow on the dreams of teachers today.

～

In His Eyes

Once, they said he was a great teacher. But with the years, the dreams in his eyes had long ago disappeared with the chalk dust of his daily classes. A teacher cannot be great without dreams. Pity the poor teacher who once had a dream, lost it, and never had another dream.

～

New Dreams

Teaching? Some call this dedication. I like to call it an insight given to each of us for some reason which we don't know. A teacher is a creator, who creates in the mind and hearts of children new worlds, new dreams, new insights. Without teachers, there can be no new worlds, no new dreams, no new insights.

We want it said of us teachers that what others thought were weeds, we nourished into prize flowers.

The Right Person

"Once upon a time . . ." and we all remember the enjoyment from the fascinating and enchanting fairy tales.

To many the story of mathematics reads more like an obituary notice rather than the vibrant story of real men and women—a story that could outsell the best seller, could outdraw the number one movie—if only the right person would make it come alive. And, each one of us can be the right person for ourselves and our students.

It should be the goal of every mathematics teacher to impart some small idea of our glorious tradition of mathematics and of the men and women who are part of that heritage and tradition.

Recognize Those Characteristics

Our task as teachers of mathematics is not to hunt for or strive for some research documented methods of achieving success in teaching the division of fractions or algorithms to facilitate the triple rule of percents. Our task is to recognize and promulgate those traits of mathematics which are truly characteristic of mathematics and which will remain permanent for all tomorrows.

If teachers could only invoke the wonders of mathematics instead of its frustrations.

~

Whether the students go on in mathematics or not, the word "math" should always remind them of warmth, enjoyment and pleasure at the achievement of the great minds and their own little but personal and treasured successes in mathematics.

~

Teachers—Be There

Be there to give them a hand when they are unsure of the way.
Be there to give them clear words when they are confused.
Be there to give them the warmth and love that they will cherish and remember and imitate for the rest of their lives.

I hope that these are not emotional words which only sting the eyes and leave the heart untouched. I hope that these are emotions that will tie a knot in your heart as a reminder each day of what your calling requires.

~

Teachers are born to shape the world we live in. This is a mandate not to be forgotten or taken lightly. Have you noticed that teachers always say, "I have to go to my classes," and never, "I have to go work." The more one loves what one is doing, the less it is called work.

~

Teaching

Teach each day as though this were to be our first day of class.
Teach each day as though this were to be our last day of class.
Teach each day as though this were to be our only day of class.

~

Teaching! This is a tremendous task to fulfill and a terrifying obligation. But it is this duality which raises teaching from an occupation to a vocation, a dedication which neither praise nor salary, neither honors nor acclaim, can generate or foster.

If teaching is not there in the heart when we begin to teach, it will never get to be there.

Advice to a Young Teacher

Go neither too slowly nor too hastily in the curriculum, there is peace and tranquillity in humoring the principal's whims.

Speak your truth clearly but carefully, and then yield to those older than you.

In your achievements be neither proud nor humble, for the meek will possess tenure.

Take kindly the ravages of time and surrender gracefully the feats of bursting youthfulness, for now a broken leg or a sprained back will not console your foolishness.

Remember, that when it is the darkest that is when the stars shine the brightest.

Above all, be at peace with yourself and the world—for there is One that watches over us all and does not need our advice on how to run His world.

The Future Doesn't Just Happen

We cannot leave the future of education just to the experts. They are not infallible. Collectively, we all have to take responsibility for the future. The future doesn't just happen. We must learn all we can from the past and use it to shape the years to come.

A teacher should be gentle but challenging, contemporary but mindful of tradition. History is our collective memory. We don't want to begin every morning not remembering yesterday. Without history, we lose our perspective.

Descartes once said, "I think, therefore I am." Our task as teachers is to teach students that because they are, they should think.

Teacher's Qualities

We need learned teachers who combine humility with scholarship.

We need professional teachers who never forget the young men and women in class, who care for and inspire the amateurs.

We need wise teachers whose goal is not to hoard wisdom but to scatter their riches with princely largess on all who come to them.

We need teachers who in all the days of their lives will only once touch the human hearts about them and cause them sorrow—that is the day that they depart this life.

I Wish . . .

One day, I would love to go back to the little red schoolhouse,
To children fresh from the hills and fields,
To children with none of the sophistication of the cities.
I would tell them about Pythagoras, Euclid, Hypatia, Plato, Aristotle, and Archimedes.
Oh, I would tell them of Gauss, Euler, Cantor, Kovalevsky, and Hilbert,
I would tell them about the wonderful heritage which is theirs.
And maybe, maybe after many years in this task,
One day one of these students in front of me would be added to the list.
I would then feel my task as a teacher fulfilled.

Teacher's Task

In the beginning, when God scattered stars into space, He bountifully hid many treasures of mind and heart for us to discover—and it is the glorious task of teachers to find these treasures and teach others to do the same.

~

First Day!

The first day I went to my classes, it was with music in my heart. Only after years in the classroom were these words added to the melodies in my heart.

I believe that:
- to touch young hearts was ever my destiny,
- to open eyes, that have seen plenty, to see greater things,
- to show hope to eyes that knew only of want,
- to teach understanding for the mind and especially for the heart,
- to teach fingers and hands that instinctively grasp and hold, to open and share and give,
- to teach the heart that is so small that it can be held in the cup of two small hands, that his heart cannot be filled by anything except infinite love.

~

Lasting Problems of Teaching

And as in the past, in our present, and for the forever future, there will be these lasting problems:

- Is there a way of teaching and transmitting the splendid, humanistic traditions of mathematics without compromising sound educational principles?
- Can the wonder of mathematics be taught with dignity, professionalism and inspiration—taught in such a way as to engender a love for mathematics and mathematics teaching?
- Can teachers share the conviction that mathematics is useful both in the intellectual order and for the necessities of a technological era, and still avoid a meaningless idealism or an all pervading vocationalism?

- Can one make the mathematics class a joyful, meaningful personal experience without engaging in the folly of extreme permissiveness?

If mathematics is everywhere around us, then mathematics should be for everyone.

- Can the teacher reach all mathematics students and not just the elite, thus meeting both the social responsibilities of teaching and the educational goals of mathematics?

Solutions to Lasting Problems

However, of one thing I am convinced: that the real teacher-leaders of now, of the new century, and for the forever future, have always known what is necessary for the todays and all the tomorrows in our classrooms.

Why? Because these teachers have inherited the inspirational tradition of teaching since teaching the young began. They know: what is needed is tenderness for who the child is and respect and wonder for what the child may become; that one cannot touch a child and not leave fingerprints on his or her mind and heart; that one should not take a complex, sensitive, reactive body like a child and treat it like a robot, teaching and preparing the child only for robots' tasks.

Human nature has not changed drastically over the centuries. The inherent curiosity of the ancients is still in every exploratory touch and grasp and look of young children. The imagination that built the seven wonders of the world is still with us in the seven million wonders in the eyes of a child. And eyes whether old or young, can never be filled with awe, amazement and wonder.

And so, besides the changes that are presently necessitated by our meteoric technological development, the structure and content of the curriculum for the future should also contain some stable, lasting, and unchanging elements of mathematics from the heritage of the past and from the glorious tradition of mathematics education.

Invocation for Teachers

Almighty God and Eternal Father, we are grateful for our blessings. Grant us insight into the problems of the day and an understanding of the means for their solution. May we who have the privilege of learning acquire knowledge without vanity and possess wisdom with humility.

We ask your blessing for:

Teachers, to whose loyalty and wisdom the young minds and hearts of children have been placed in trust during impressionable years;

These men and women whose destiny is leadership, and who open a new dimension in the world of the young mind, who in the straight jacket of a professional vocabulary can introduce an extraordinary intimacy, gentleness, devotion, and inspiration;

Men and women with deep personal and prayerful hope in the future of your children and who make of their work not the beating drudgery of a job but the exultation of a vocation.

Give them wisdom for moments of decision and destroy all complacency in teaching and personal achievement.

For those under our care, we also pray:

Bestow upon them the wisdom of maturity though their minds be young;

Give them the understanding of age though their hearts be youthful;

Grant them your eternal love to share in a mortal heart with all men and women in a world where only love can restore your peace and their happiness.

Amen

Chapter 4
Teacher's Challenge

Oracle at Delphi

Long ago in ancient Greece, the Oracle at Delphi answered knowledgeably and wisely all the questions proposed by those who came for advice. The Oracle was revered by all—well, almost by all. Demetrios remained a skeptic and a doubter of the powers and wisdom of the Oracle.

One day, Demetrios decided to test the great Oracle and hopefully to trap it into a wrong statement.

He would take a very small bird to the Oracle and hold it hidden in his cupped hands.

He would ask the Oracle: "What do I have in my hands?" Demetrios was sure that this much the Oracle would know and answer: "A bird."

Demetrios would then ask: "Is it alive or dead?"

If the Oracle said it was dead, Demetrios would release the live bird. If the Oracle said it was alive, he would crush the bird to death and so prove the Oracle wrong.

The day came when Demetrios stood before the Oracle at Delphi and asked: "What do I hold in my cupped hands?"

The Oracle replied: "A bird."

Demetrios then continued: "Is it alive or dead?"
There was a pause, and then the Oracle responded: "The answer to that question, is in YOUR HANDS."

And so your happiness as a teacher is also in your hands. It can be crushed and destroyed. It can be made to live each day of your life.

Perhaps the most tragic of all teachers are the ones who go to class without joy, depart without sorrow, and retire without regret, teachers for whom classes should have been full of immortal moments to treasure and remember, when remembering is all that they have left.

∽

On the first day of my teaching career, I had an accident—I bumped into reality.

∽

What does it take to become dedicated? How does one acquire the spirit of dedication? The answer is well known and simple. It is love, love of what one is doing and love of doing it for someone.

∽

Lost Motivation

A famous psychologist summarized his many experiences with people who had lost motivation in their lives by stating: these people had no reason to get up the next morning, each morning was the same
    as the one before,
    as the one today, and certainly,
    as the one tomorrow.
And then, one day they will find no motivation to get up at all.

∽

There are those who spend today wondering if they'll have a tomorrow—and when the day comes when there is no tomorrow, they have had neither today nor tomorrow.

∽

Only Today Is Certain

You know—the good God has promised us everything, every-
thing on earth.
Except one thing—
He did not promise us a tomorrow for our procrastination.
And so as teachers—
We, who have so much to give to the young, to give and give
each day—
We cannot delay, we cannot put off our giving till tomorrow,
No matter how tired, weary, frustrated we may be today—
For we have not been promised a tomorrow—we only have
today.

When at the end of the day, someone asks me, "Are you tired?"
I'm still too much of a teacher and I ask, "Of what?"

The dream is in our hearts, the fulfillment is in our hands.

Dreams

Most of us have dreams:
* young ones which we give up with time,
* older ones which we learn to be but dreams,
* and the one that persists, the one that could be realized.

My Life, a Dream

I said I wanted to be a teacher!
And now, they said,
My life would be
A dream away from all reality.

How I Knew?

"They asked me how I knew that my love was true?"

I, who walked with a leash of love each day hungrily seeking for the underdog.

"How did I know that my love was true?"

I, who felt the hunger of each child in me and shared tears with the hurt and the forlorn.

And then they knew that my love was true.

Greatness? It is measured by the causes to which one dedicates a life—and there is no cause greater than the teaching and improvement of children.

The teacher tired and exhausted at the end of the day in the kindergarten classroom. And her reward? From one of her charges a shy grin, a thank you, and a kiss. Teaching would not be worth a life, if it were not for this.

They tell of the beginning teacher who walked into the principal's office after two weeks of teaching and said, "Gimme that inspirational speech again, I'm getting discouraged."

Medically Confirmed

There are teachers who have merely thought and thought about doing something and have never done anything.

Why?

It is medically confirmed that in the process of thinking, blood is drawn from the feet to the brain—and if all you do is just think about something, you'll always get cold feet.

Teacher's Tears

A teacher's tears are:

- for joy and sadness,
- for disappointment and pain,
- for partings and loneliness,
- but most of all for pride.

A teacher who, as her students graduate or when she reads about their achievements, can cry with a smile in her eyes.

Teacher's Joy

A teacher's joy is to know that the spark in their students fanned through the years into a brilliant flame was kindled by their fire.

What was one of my thrills in teaching? Making a child smile from performing a task successfully.

Maybe a lifetime is not sufficient to thank those who give a lifetime to and for others. But the dedication goes on with or without thanks. And one day, the teachers will have taught all to be teachers—not of hoary disciplines like reading, writing, and 'rithmetic, but to be teachers of love for each other.

To be a teacher is to be unafraid of the truth, of any truth and to wish it to be known by all.

What is a teacher? Someone who lives a brief moment of inspiration every moment.

Good-byes

When she said her good-byes at the end of the school year, her eyes were shining with the highlight that tears will make when one does not permit them to fall.

Teacher Going to Class Each Day

Why do I go to class each day?
Because my heart is with the young.
My heart so vulnerable to the young with their sorrows and their tears,
My heart so aglow to the young with their laughter and their joys,
My heart that they will always know and have with them—
For whenever they look into theirs—there is where they'll always find my own.

The teachers who row the boat seldom have the time or energy to rock it. This is the salvation of the sometimes inefficient administration within our schools.

The one who has imagination soars on the wings of eagles.

Excellence? You must develop it for yourself—it cannot be imitated or copied like a painting.

One of our great consolations is the fact that all disappointments are finite.

Anonymous Treasury

Teachers are not concerned that their names be remembered. Their hope is to contribute a little to the anonymous treasury which will filter down to succeeding generations and add to the sum total of right values by which people live.

In a school, only one thing is necessary to have a happy class—a happy teacher.

Totally Committed

If you don't want to be a math teacher, by all means find work in some other profession. The classroom frustration and social rejection can be endured only if the math teacher is totally committed.

People need incentives in order to work harder. What incentives does the American school system provide its teachers?

In many instances, if it wasn't for the wholehearted commitment of individual teachers, the educational system in America would come to a complete standstill.

What kind of teachers can go on day after day with the daily schedule?

Teachers whose inner energies are fueled by love.

The teacher passes on the wonder and awe of his or her own mind to pupils and in so doing renews it within, again and again.

Good Teachers

Obviously, good teachers give far more of themselves than mere instruction in a subject. They give heart and courage, confidence and inspiration to the growing, malleable youths entrusted to their care.

And this giving continues day after day. And sometimes, perhaps a little discouraged, one asks, "Must I keep giving and giving forever?"

And the answer is no, only until you yourself stop receiving from the Master.

For every teacher to read and remember:

> "I heard the voice of the Lord saying, 'Whom shall I send and who will go for us?'
> Then I said, 'Here I am, send me!'"
> Isaiah 6:8.

Some of us rarely have the opportunity to see the full extent of human effort spent by those teachers who are passionately dedicated to getting something done well. When such commitment is also accompanied by imagination and creativity in the performance of the task, it leaves the observer with gratitude and inspiration.

The essential characteristic of dedication and sacrifice is that they claim nothing in return. One can learn these from parents and patriots, but especially from teachers.

Teacher's Beliefs

I depend:
- on the chairperson for tasks assigned me,
- on the principal for my job,
- on the superintendent for the continuation of my job,
- on the school committee for the very existence of my job.

But I depend:
- on my love for children to continue to be with them,
- on my integrity to teach them as best I can,
- on my honesty to teach them the truth as we both find it,
- on my devotion to care for the children entrusted to me,
- on my enthusiasm to inspire children to a lifelong habit of learning.

Treasures from Each Day

What treasures do I bring home from class each day?

- Oh frequently, a smudged and wrinkled homework page with "I love you" written small at the bottom of the page.
- Many a time, my palm still sticky from the spontaneous grasp of the little boy who pulled me away from the other children to show me a grasshopper he had caught just before coming to school.
- Always a wrinkle in my shirt from the embrace of a little one who responded to my warm smile.

And then there is the little misgiving that I have not given the class what they have given me—so that in fitful sleep, I long to have the night pass quickly and peacefully and bring me another day to be again with the children, as soon as possible. Thus I gather my treasure each day—and long for days without end.

Teachers' Frustration Room

Besides a teachers' lounge in each school, there ought to be a teachers' frustration room—a place where a teacher can go
- and yell,
- and scream,
- and pound and kick the walls and then,
- be silent,
- meditate,
- and learn from silence a wisdom that does not often appear in the lounge unless older teachers are there.

The difference in teachers is easily recognized: some teachers get emotional about children, while great teachers get involved with them.

~

Why Be a Teacher?

I looked for the answer in the teaching of the schools of education—and it was not there,

I looked for the answer in increased salaries, the benefits and promised security given by the school board—and it was not there,

I looked for the answer in the activities of the teacher unions—and it was not there,

Finally, I looked for the answer in the hearts of dedicated teachers who make teaching their vocation and not the beating drudgery of a job—and I found it there.

~

Each teacher marches to a personal drummer. But this is the beauty and the glory of teaching. Though there may be one thousand drummers, there is but one beat in the heart of every teacher.

~

Darn Sight Easier

A teacher visited an insane asylum. One of the inmates asked, "They say that you're a teacher."

"Yes," said the teacher.

The inmate continued, "Have you ever been crazy?"

"Why, no," answered the teacher.

In a whisper the inmate added, "Try it, it's a darn sight easier than teaching."

~

The world needs teachers with adventurous, searching imaginations, teachers who love mathematics. Then no matter what the problems, they will be solved. For the one who loves, all is possible. For the one who does not love, even the possible becomes impossible.

~

As long as you laugh, who cares why.

~

Teachers in the Morning

With mind and body rested and nerves not yet tested,
We can face a class with calm and forbearance.
But the steady drain on energy and willpower,
Caused by repeated annoyances as the hours pass,
Make some teachers time bombs with short fuses.
Teachers have infinite patience
But not that infinite on some days.

~

Child's Needs

And what does the child need?
I know it all by heart after twenty years of teaching.
The child needs to be accepted, respected, liked, and trusted.
The child needs to be encouraged, supported, activated, amused.
The child needs to explore, experiment, and achieve.
And so many a time I've gone to my room, closed the door, and shouted at the walls,
"The child needs so much and I have so little to give.

All I lack is:
- Solomon's wisdom,
- the gentleness of a dove,
- the patience of Job,
- Einstein's knowledge,
- Florence Nightingale's dedication,
- the persistence of the Devil."

I feel like grabbing the child and saying, "You demand more from me than you do from your parents."

But you know, the child may be right in this. Parents are responsible only for the child's life,

But I, I as the child's teacher, am responsible for the kind of life the child will live.

~

It is only after years of teaching that I finally realized that just because students ask questions, it doesn't always mean they want to hear the answers.

~

Once you succeed in making students think, there is the temptation to make them all think alike. Unfortunately, to think means to think differently from everybody else.

~

The Old Teacher and the Young Teacher

The young teacher walked by the classroom and watched day by day as the old teacher took the child and struggled for hours to teach the child some simple arithmetic.

Finally, one day the young teacher interrupted the old teacher and asked, "Why do you do this day after day?"

The old teacher answered, "So that the child will learn and know."

"But," the young teacher replied, "there are so many like this one in this same situation. How can your efforts with just one student make any difference?"

The old teacher looked at his pupil and continued with the lesson. To the young teacher he simply said, "It makes a difference to this one."

~

Teachers

We are not like ships that pass through the waves and leave no mark of their passing.

We are not like birds that fly through the air and leave no proof of their coming and going.

We have left a stamp on the minds of our young students and many years from now, our fleeting moment here, will be recognized in someone we have never seen and never will see, and people's hearts will be glad.

We are vulnerable men and women haunted and obsessed by time, neither anticipating nor expecting greatness—just devoted hearts dedicated to duty.

∼ *Interlude* ∼
School Daze

First grade was very frustrating for me. I couldn't read or write and the teacher wouldn't let me talk. I didn't have a very happy childhood, but thank God, it's been a nice long one.

I loved second grade arithmetic, which I recited with great conviction and no understanding.

In the third grade, I also learned that if you spit on the rubber end of your pencil you can erase ink. It disappears with the hole in the paper.

One of my thrills in the fifth grade arithmetic class was to watch the teacher turn decimals into fractions.

When I was in the sixth grade in parochial school, we had a teacher who I'm sure invented fear. We called her "Attila the Nun."

I was fortunate to have had teachers with mind and heart open to the things that come from the imagination of a young boy. I was often encouraged, corrected, and chastised—and all were necessary for growth.

I received great comfort and consolation from scripture when in school. I also learned not to study. "The Lord is my shepherd. . . ."

Do sheep have to study?

The first time I found out that a "little learning is a dangerous thing" was when I brought my first report card home to Dad.

I tangled with my algebra teacher very early in the course. She used to walk into class and begin with, "Let x be any number."

One day I raised my hand and said, "Let 4 be any letter." She did not like that at all, nor did she care for me.

My teacher told me I aggravated her a great deal and the greatest aggravation was my perfect attendance in her class.

I will never forget my father on my college graduation day. There I was resplendent in cap and gown and my father shouting at me: "What do you mean you still want to be a cowboy!"

I could have easily discovered the calculus like Newton and also his law of gravitation. You see, I've watched apple trees, and I've seen apples fall. The only difference between me and Newton is that I picked up the apples and ate them. Newton asked why they fell.

In algebra class in high school, I was told to put arrow heads on the coordinate axes.

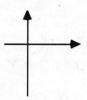

I exercised quite a bit of originality in college. I added feathers.

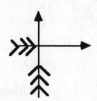

Chapter 5
Teaching is a Vocation

A Teacher's Creed

I believe that my position in a school as a teacher is not a job but a vocation—a calling that has singled me out for this special task.

I believe that I cannot touch these minds and hearts of children and not leave fingerprints on their impressionable minds and sensitive hearts.

I believe that I must give my students what I myself need—love and tolerance for mistakes, patience and compassion for occasional failures, a word of encouragement instead of a casual put-down.

I believe that the bright and the slow, the quick and those who only plod are my special care. I must encourage both to reach for the stars—for it is not a hopeless goal for any of them.

I believe that I must encourage my students not only to follow the visions of the mind but also to share the treasures of the heart.

I believe that some day I will find out why I have been singled out for my teaching vocation. This one thing I know now:

I was given this gift of love and faith in the young at birth.
It was the star that I would follow all the days of my life.

A young teacher is a companion, a confidant.
An older teacher is stability, peace and security.

Humpty Dumpty

We all have Humpty-Dumptys in the classroom—those who are so fragile and yet so precious. We must see that they do not tumble down. "O little wandering spirit, please stay in one piece."

There are no carrots big enough, none juicy enough, there are no sticks big enough to force recalcitrants into the educational line.

I had a rash so I went to a dermatologist. He looked at me and asked, "When were you last in a jungle?"
I answered, "This morning in PS 148."

In the ever present economic crunch, teachers are always inadequately paid. But I am also convinced that there is no amount of money that will make a teacher care for children just as there is no amount of money that can adequately repay a teacher for caring.

With a little encouragement, a young mind will know no bounds to what it can see and do.

As teachers, we often deal with average Americans who face loneliness, disintegrating self-esteem, stress, fear, old age, and unreasonable demands to succeed.

I could never see why my teacher favored Bert. He was clever and very bright. But who isn't?

High IQ ≠ Giftedness

There is the questionable notion that a high IQ is synonymous with giftedness. It only tells us that person has the potential for gifted behavior, but unless intelligence is combined with creativity and dedication and shows up in performance, there is no rationale for assuming that a student with simply a high IQ is gifted.

Geniuses are easy to recognize—they light their own fires.

There is one minority group which we invariably neglect in our schools—the minority group of the very talented students.

The gifted? They are some confused students who copy our mysterious codes from the blackboard and can give it back on the test.

There are two types of wonderful students in my class:
- One type thinks math is Wonderful,
- The other type thinks that math is Wonder-Full.

A jumper cable for students who are slow starters is in every classroom—it's called "teacher."

Failure for a teacher does not come from not opening a student's mind as much as not opening his heart.

Loss

We all can understand and help people who lose their minds, but nothing, nothing in the world can make us understand the people who lose their hearts.

Teaching is often as glamorous as crawling on your stomach in a snake pit.

Who is a good teacher? Someone who is good at understanding those who are not so good at explaining, and is good at explaining to those not so good at understanding.

Who first formed the words for loyalty, devotion, and love? It must have been teachers for they valued these virtues and wanted others to imitate them as long as they lived.

I am preparing my students to live—not only to make a living. The subject matter is a subtle medium through which I try to tell them how.

Invitation for a Teacher: This Could Happen to You

The teacher did not remember the student's many mistakes, but only the fact that the student had tried so hard. The teacher did recall the student's grade should have been much lower than the one received.

So you can imagine the teacher's surprise years later upon receiving an invitation to a party for the Nobel Laureate.

Instill a Belief

What was college math like?

Some of it was very much like high school math. It was watch, do, and tell. I did have a teacher who did not do much to teach me how to think or reason logically—but he did give me one priceless heritage.

He instilled in me a firm belief that I could reason—and that if I did think and think clearly—the answers in the back of the book didn't matter.

For the first time, I dared to submit an answer to a problem that disagreed with the one given by the author of my textbook.

My teacher had wonderful confidence in my abilities. One day she said, "Sit down and play the piano."

I said, "But, I don't know how to play the piano!"

She looked at me and said, "How do you know until you sit down?"

Teachers very often see in students the potential that the students do not see in themselves.

Not All of Us

I think that what is lacking in mathematics teachers is a sense of humor—the ability to look at ourselves in stark reality. We are neither divine nor immortal nor full of wisdom—at least not all of us.

The most dangerous time in sailing for going off course is when the winds are most favorable. The same is true for all teachers in their daily tasks.

Reach for a Star

During a National Council of Teachers of Mathematics meeting in one of our large cities, I came out of the last afternoon session on a Friday and walked into the hotel lobby.

A rather jovial and expansive fellow with an o-be-joyful glass in his hand looked at the NCTM badge on my suit lapel.

Turning to me he asked, "Say Padre, is there some kind of conference here?"

"Yes," I answered, "and as a matter of fact a very important one."

"Who are the people attending the convention?" he asked.

"They're teachers," I answered.

Somewhat curious he asked, "And what do these teachers teach?"

I gave the obvious answer, "They teach children."

He continued, "And what do they teach the children?"

"How to reach a star," I replied.

At this he blinked, looked at me puzzled, and then asked as though he had not heard me correctly, "Reach a what?"

"A star," I repeated.

With amazement that reflected his meager knowledge of the purpose of education, he asked, "But who would want that?"

I looked at him hoping that perhaps just for a moment, he would recall and recapture his own youth and his classroom teachers. I continued, "Children will always want to reach a star, and when the day comes when they don't want to reach a star, that will be the day when there are no more children."

At this, the fellow took a sip out of his glass, nodded, and walked away.

A Universe of Order
This infant hand so tenderly small!
Strong only to brush a tear,
Or hold a kiss—or hide in fear.
Yet waved in sleepy farewell to the skies
Makes the night stars tremble
And leave twinkles in those soft blue eyes.

Your name as a "teacher" will still be revered and praised when the pyramids are dust.

A teacher's love for students may not outshine the stars, but it will still be there when there are no more stars.

The young, you will notice, are always jumping up. Some jump higher and higher—way up into the sky—never happy with how high they jump. If they can't be stars, they will never be happy with any height.

Stars
My teacher was old.
And I've been told
She couldn't teach
What a child must reach.
But to this day
I can only pray
That others may
Look back and say—
That once in their youth
Someone in love with truth,
Had a gift that understood
Not the mind but the heart
And in class,
Scattered handfuls of stars.

The student complained wistfully to the teacher,

"I never see the charm, the beauty, the magic of mathematics that you see—I never see the things you see."

There is only one response for the teacher, "That's why I'm here, to teach you so that you can see."

We need teachers who will bring to young minds the thrill and perpetual adventure of learning and who will keep youthful eyes alight with eternal wonder.

Teacher's Traits

What traits must a teacher possess? Nothing more than friendship, kindness, patience and loyalty, understanding, a share of laughter, and a great deal of faith and trust.

Teachers Are Guides

An Alpine guide is precisely that, a guide and should not be a part of the mountain which is the obstacle to be conquered by the climber. The same analogy applies to teachers; they are and should remain guides.

As a teacher, lead, follow, or get out of the way.

As teachers, we shine a light into a dark tunnel, but at the end, the student must walk the tunnel alone.

A teacher is like a candle burning with light for all until it is no more.

The teacher can light the candle and put it in a student's hand. But the student must walk into the dark alone.

∼

A teacher's lines around the eyes reflect not age, but wisdom garnered from study far, far into the night.

∼

To be a teacher is to be a genius—for who else could house, feed, and clothe a family on a teacher's salary.

∼

To some people much is given—of other people much is expected. And those other people are teachers.

∼

As teachers, we always admire the precocious student who is bright enough to ask our advice.

∼

Rising Sun

A teacher walks into the classroom each day like the rising sun bursting with light to be received and cherished, with warmth to be enjoyed and remembered, when the days are dark and cold.

∼

Among the many marvelous rediscoveries of our age has been the fact that students vary in ability and interests. The result is individualized learning. Let the teachers match the students. There are teachers who can handle the slow and the underachiever, inspire the recalcitrant, and move the non-learner.

∼

Distinguishing characteristics—an immature teacher imitates, a mature teacher steals!

∼

An effective teacher does the right things. An efficient teacher does the things right.

~

What is teaching? Teaching is love shared with students.

~

Love of the classroom is not an art that teachers acquire—it is their life.

~

Many a teacher has wondered how one could get so far behind in one lifetime.

~

Teachers find out rather quickly that students are much more difficult to shepherd than sheep.

~

Work and Play

There are at least two kinds of play for children:
- one physical like running and throwing or kicking a ball,
- the other, the play of imagination at various levels and one of these levels is that of mathematics.

One would not reasonably advocate the abolition of work and the substitution of play for it, although that would be quite a good idea were it not for the fact that you cannot force anyone to play. You can force them to work—but not to play.

Play is possible only when some internal mechanism is properly tuned. And so we are like musicians, hoping to strike a responsive chord in the minds and hearts of our students.

Brilliant pupils may appear so, only because by good luck their minds resonate with our own, but even poor students can often resonate with our minds, if we provide enough mathematical variety. And when that happens, we have good teaching and effective learning.

One teacher to another:

"Don't you wish you could destroy that rebellious, obnoxious brat in your class?"

First teacher:

"Oh, I did. I made him my friend."

Teachers wipe out ignorance one child at a time.

Impatience

I rarely get impatient with my students. Why should I get impatient with them when I am infinitely patient with my own stupidity?

Teachers in the classroom often get upset about the little things. Why shouldn't they? After all, germs kill more people than dinosaurs.

A Lesson in Economics
Location: Smalltown, USA

A community built a new one-classroom schoolhouse.

"Well," the residents said, "If we have a schoolhouse, then we better have a teacher."

So they hired a teacher. Then someone said, "A teacher needs a salary."

So they hired an accountant. But the accountant pointed out that they now needed a treasurer.

So they hired a treasurer. With a teacher, an accountant, and treasurer the people all agreed that they had to have an administrator to direct the group.

The residents of the community appointed an administrator. But lo and behold, the legislature then voted a cut in educational funding and so school personnel had to be cut back.

The residents fired the teacher.

Many of the ills of American education can be traced to the loss of hunger for learning.

When School Closes

Failure in teaching occurs when a child's mind closes when school closes. Teaching should train a child for a lifetime of learning.

I bury my message in humor and sometimes in tears.

No teacher should ever make the mistake that what has to be learned has necessarily to be taught.

Respect and Affection

Good teachers know that it is the student who is learning, and we are there to help, not by being the center of attraction, but by guidance, stimulation, encouragement, and a humaneness that projects itself into a lifetime of mutual respect. Respect for children must precede affectionate hand-holding. And with respect and affection there must be the presence of skills on the part of the teacher, if children are to be helped to learn.

Anyone can be a success if one has no regard for values—the problem is to be a success with a set of values.

Teachers! If you can't make leaders out of your students, then teach them which leaders to follow.

Understanding students is not in the head, but in the heart.

A Teacher's Prayer

When I face the Lord's computer, I hope it can be told that though I'm spindled and mutilated, I didn't fold.

A child's early life is lived in the heart, not in the head, and the most important thing you can do as a teacher is to foster the love in that heart for learning.

Teachers' Concerns

As teachers, we should be concerned that mathematics be understood, appreciated, and even enjoyed by the slow, the average, the reluctant, the unmotivated, the disenchanted, the disinterested, the bright—by as many students as possible. The basic problem of all students is essentially the same—they need to have their curiosity stimulated, their interest aroused and their enthusiasm kindled.

~ *Interlude* ~
Summer Employment

People outside the teaching profession do not always share the same opinion about its value that we do. I learned this in my youth.

After graduating from Boston College, I looked for a summer job at Filene's, a large department store. The personnel director was slow in coming to a decision.

Finally he said, "Okay, you can have the job. Here's a broom, now go sweep the floors."

I protested, "But sir, I'm a college grad."

With sheer disgust, he looked at me and said, "All right, I'll show you how."

I also applied for a summer job at Jordan Marsh. The personnel director asked me what my credentials were. I thought they were rather impressive. I had had: 10 years of Latin, 8 years of Greek, 3 years of philosophy, 4 years of theology, and I even sneaked in a year of Hebrew.

The personnel director looked at me and said, "Sorry son, I can't use you, but I'll tell you what: you'd make a helluva good Roman Emperor!"

Chapter 6
Students

Wonder of "What If?"

As teachers, our presumption to teach carries with it an assumption

- that we never stop studying,
- that we never stop questioning and searching,
- that we never stop wondering, "What if?"

And so often a child will ask, "If the world were made of ice cream, would it melt?"

As adults, we answer with logic, "But dear, the world isn't made of ice cream."

A child never stops asking, "What if?"

And the child is constantly being told, "But it isn't."

It is so easy to stifle the curiosity, the imagination and the creativity in the minds of the young.

The young need sanctuaries for imaginative thinking,
For the multiplicity of visions and dreams,

That for them are images of potential tomorrows.

I love to talk with children. I can often predict some conversations with adults long before their conclusion. But the words of children, though they may be the same as those of adults, are put together so as to startle me into perpetual wonder.

A student's thoughts during a difficult examination in mathematics: "When I consider how many other problems there are which I cannot solve and yet have learned to live with, these ten problems here will not cause me any more trouble."

~

Love, Not Argue

We had a busy and tiring day in class.
At the end of it, he came to me,
Threw his arms around me and said,
"I love you."
I remembered one-upsmanship.
"Oh, I bet I love you more than you love me."
He looked up and simply said,
"I want to love you, not argue with you."

~

The Little Imp

She was an imp.
"What is five times seven?" I asked.
"Do you know the answer?"
"Of course."
"Then isn't it enough that one of us knows the answer?"
"Well, what would you want me to ask you?"
"Something that you don't know."

~

Frankie

Frankie was not the fastest youngster in my class. Never did he come up with the right answer, rarely did he raise his hand. One day we were factoring quadratics. I put the problem $x^2 + 2x + 1 = 0$ on the board for factoring. Frankie raised his hand. I was elated. "What do we do here?" I asked.

Frankie responded, "Find the y-intercept."

~

A Battle of Wits

I did some teaching and classroom visitations at the Cleary School in Providence, Rhode Island. I lost every battle of wits with the students except one. It happened this way.

One day, I was in the kindergarten and asked the class, "What shall we do today?"

"Draw pictures," a youngster said.

"All right," I answered, "What do you want me to draw?"

"Draw a dog," said the youngster.

Oh, I thought I had him. I knew he was too young to be able to say Dalmatian, Dachshund, or Saint Bernard, so I asked, "What kind of a dog do you want me to draw."

He replied, "Draw a red dog."

I drew something that only remotely resembled a dog and I asked, "What does a dog say?"

The class shouted, "Bow-wow." Someone else said, "Draw a cow."

My cow had square legs and one had to have an unusual imagination to see a cow in my drawing. I asked, "What does a cow say?"

"Moo-moo," answered the class. Then a little girl said, "Draw a giant."

I had her! I said, "But dear, the board isn't big enough to draw a giant."

She just looked at me smilingly, and said, "Draw a small giant." Next, a boy said, "Draw a chicken."

The only thing that resembled a chicken in my drawing was the beak since I drew this many times in geometry as the symbol for an angle. The rest was a mess.

The boy looked at the picture and said, "That's a funny looking chicken."

At this I replied, "You're right, because you see, I wanted to know if you were alert. That's not a chicken, it happens to be an eagle."

"An eagle?" said the boy.

"Yup," I answered.

The boy continued with, "What does an eagle say?"

For the first and only time in my life I had an inspiration. I patted the boy on the head and said, "An eagle says, *E Pluribus Unum*!" With that I left the classroom in a hurry.

～

A Trick Question

A few days before a test, a student asked me, "Are there going to be any trick questions on the test?"

"What do you mean by 'trick questions'?" I asked.

He replied, "You know, questions where you have to think."

～

Open Book Test

I told my students that the test next week was going to be an "open book" test. One student asked me what that meant. I said, "You can use your book."

He looked at me and asked, "What book?"

～

Student to teacher:
"Don't explain it to me. Just show me how to do it and get the answer."

～

A Serious Question

The Roman collar is not what children in the early grades are used to seeing and especially during the arithmetic period. I walked into the fourth grade while the class was doing problems in multiplication.

One little boy looked up and asked, "Who are you?"

"I'm a Jesuit," I answered.

He looked unimpressed and continued with, "What's that?"

I explained to him that Jesuits are priests who work in parishes, and teach in high schools, colleges, and universities. I added that we were also missionaries and that as a matter of fact, we came to America about one hundred twenty-five years ago.

Very seriously, the boy asked, "Were you one of them?"

I told a joke in a class in an elementary school. No one laughed. Later, I asked one of the girls why no one laughed. She shook her head, and said, "We're in the fourth grade now."

It Only Took Four Weeks

During one school visit a teacher told me that one of the youngsters in the first grade was not keen on arithmetic. So I talked to the youngster. I asked, "How long have you been in school?"

He said, "Four weeks."

"And you don't like arithmetic?" I asked.

"Naw, it's no good. I'm sorry I learned it."

Gina

I asked, "What is 2 + 3?" and waited for students to raise their hands.

I asked, "What is 2 + 3?" and called on Gina. She blurted out, "You can't call on me, I didn't raise my hand."

Teacher comes up in back of a student in study hall. "Why aren't you studying?" the teacher asks.

Student answers, "'Cause I didn't see you coming."

School Prayer

Prayer of a student before an exam:

> "Now I lay me down to rest,
> I hope I pass tomorrow's test.
> If I should die before I wake,
> That's one less test I'll have to take."

To be with children is to live in a time of eternal spring.

The Hares and the Tortoises

I visited a third grade classroom recently. There were slow students and fast students in the class. The teacher called the slow students, "The Hares," and the fast ones, "The Tortoises." I cornered one of the boys and said, "You are called a hare. Now hares are fast but you work slowly, don't you?"

"My whole group is slow," he said.

"Does anyone else know about this besides you?" I asked.

"We all do," he answered.

"Why don't you tell the teacher then?" I countered.

"She called us hares not to hurt our feelings, why should we hurt hers?" was his reply.

A young boy sneezes directly in front of himself and his teacher says, "Sneeze the other way."

The boy responds, "This is the only way I know."

After discussing some problems in number theory, I assigned twelve problems to a class of fifth graders. About ten minutes later, one of the students came to the desk and asked, "Do you have any more problems?"

Quite surprised, I said, "Do you mean to tell me that you have already solved the problems I gave you?"

The student answered, "Well, actually I couldn't solve any of them, I thought you might have some problems I could solve."

Child with Rainbow

One winter morning a young child bundled up and went out into the December cold. Soon it began to snow. The snowflakes fell on her long black lashes. She saw the world through rainbows, and that's the way she has looked at the world ever since.

Young children's logic:
There are printed words in books and there are books with pictures. Printed words are for people who can't read pictures.

Throughout my years of teaching, I have always been puzzled by the mystery and the promise in the development of my young students.

The students that are interesting are the ones that are interested.

Children do not wonder at miracles. They are aware of them and believe in them. That is why children achieve miracles while we adults only marvel at miracles.

Children often experience loneliness; they are not old enough to appreciate solitude.

∼

Billy

First grade did not always agree with Billy. And so there were plenty of tears. The kind teacher remembered her own days of fright and loneliness and understood. She let Billy's tears stop and dry in their own time.

∼

Mary Sue

As I walked into a first grade, I saw Mary Sue counting pegs one by one. I asked her how many pegs she had. She said, "Twelve."

I asked her to count the pegs again, only this time to count them by twos. Mary Sue answered, "Fourteen."

I asked if there were twelve or fourteen. She answered, "There are twelve pegs if you count by ones and fourteen pegs if you count by twos."

∼

How Long Have You Been . . .

A visiting teacher to a school watching a second grader struggling with an arithmetic problem asked, "How long have you been in the second grade?"

"Two months," said the youngster and continued with a question for the teacher, "How long have you been in school?"

Somewhat taken aback the teacher said, "Ten years."

"It's hell, ain't it?" responded the youngster sympathetically.

∼

From a student essay:
> "Mathematics is much nicer than an automobile accident, a tight girdle, a higher income tax bracket, or a holding pattern over Chicago. But sometimes I doubt it."

∼

The Collar

I was in a hotel in Portland, Maine registering for a New England mathematics conference. A little boy was standing with his mother who was also registering for the meeting. The boy kept staring at me and finally he tugged at his mother's coat and in a voice that echoed throughout the lobby asked, "Mom, why is that man wearing a flea collar?"

That Trick of Yours

Years ago, I gave a talk in a small town schoolhouse located far away from any cities. A boy from the backwoods, who had never been to school before, came to listen. He sat enthralled during class. Afterwards, I met him and asked if he enjoyed the lesson.

"Certainly did." he answered.

"What did you like best?" I asked.

"Well," he said, "that trick of yours when you waved the brush over the board and all those white marks disappeared."

Teacher tells a little girl to go stand at the end of the line. In no time she is back. The teacher asks, "Why didn't you do as I told you?"

"I couldn't," said the girl, "there was somebody there already."

A student, after struggling with Fermat's Last Theorem remarked: "As far as I'm concerned, Fermat's Last Theorem is also my last mathematics theorem."

Tommy

What shall I say about young Tommy?

- Noisy mostly, but his shouting could turn to whispers if he wished so.
- Unpredictable almost always, yet always doing the right thing when needed.
- A trace of shyness and a blend of pride.
- A little stubborn, with a puppy's whim to test his master's rule.
- His soft brown eyes could well up in tears and be dried by bubbling laughter.

Oh, Tommy was wild and he was gentle.

- He was good and he was bad.
- He was often happy and sometimes sad.
- He was in love with all things on earth and in the skies, But mostly, he was a little boy in love with his teacher.

He came to me and asked a question. In response, I said, "I don't know. What you are asking is the eternal question."

He looked sheepish and asked, "Since when?"

A teacher can learn many things from children, for instance, how much patience she or he has.

The one thing that can always shake a teacher is a display of common sense.

New teacher:

"Cara, what is two pears and three pears?"

Cara:

"I don't know; we've only done sums with apples."

Seen the Truth

Student after a complicated lecture in advanced calculus states: "I have seen the truth, and I'm sure I can live my life without it."

Homework Helper

Janek came home from school late and his father asked, "Why did the teacher keep you after school?"

Janek replied, "It was all your fault."

"What do you mean it was all my fault?" asked his father.

"Well, remember last night when I was doing my homework and I asked you how much is a million dollars—well, 'a helluva lot' was not the right answer."

Principal:

"Does the first grade teacher talk to herself when she's alone?"

First grader:

"Can't say. I've never been with her when she's alone."

A child's use of statistics is wonderful—"But everyone can stay out until 1:00 a.m." This is based on a sample of one, the one living in the next house.

A young boy was asked to name two days of the week that begin with T. He answered brightly and quickly, "Today and tomorrow!"

Find Angle A

Takeo Yamura worked with an educational TV station in Tokyo, Japan. He wrote me and asked if I could arrange to get him one hundred or so sixth graders to participate in an assessment project. He planned to administer a common mathematics test in Tokyo, the USA, and France to get some idea of what mathematics sixth graders knew in these three countries.

When Mr. Yamura arrived in the USA, I had 169 sixth graders in a school gymnasium ready to take the test. We gave out the test papers. The following was one of the questions:

Find angle A.

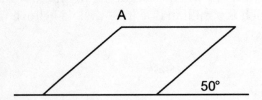

Now the supplementary angle of 50° is 130°. Opposite angles of a parallelogram are congruent and so angle A is 130°.

I watched a boy working on this problem. He first scratched his head, chewed his pencil, looked at me and smiled, and looked around the gymnasium at the other students. Then he returned to the problem.

After two or three minutes, his eyes lit up like neon bulbs. With his pencil, he drew a big arrow on the figure and wrote:

Find angle A.

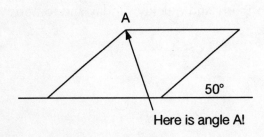

Here is angle A!

Remember the many test questions of the type:
Expand: $(2x + 3)^3$
One student had no difficulty with this problem.

$$(2x + 3)^3$$

$$(2x + 3)^3$$

$$(2x + 3)^3$$

$$(2x + 3)^3$$

And the test question:

Reduce: $\dfrac{8}{10}$

Again, this particular student had no difficulty.

$$\frac{8}{10}$$

$$\frac{8}{10}$$

$$\frac{8}{10}$$

$$\frac{8}{10}$$

Unquestionably, one source of difficulty with our mathematics is our misuse of language.

Tony

One day in class, I said to Tony, "We'll write 1 x 2 x 3 x 4 as 4!"
Tony's comment was, "Boy, that's clever."

Every time my students multiply two five digit numbers in two ways—using first one of the numbers as a multiplier and then the other—they refute the commutative property of multiplication.

A student's observation:

"Abstract mathematics? It's mathematics with all traces of reality out of it."

The wise man said, "There is always room at the top."
The student wondered, "Then why is there so much shoving going on up there?"

Students do not necessarily relate to problems based on the needs of adult life. Any problem that attracts the students is real life and real world for them.

There are some students for whom the most convincing argument why they should study mathematics is: It is a fascinating game!

Patterns of Thought

The actions a student takes to solve a problem seldom are born of the moment. They usually come from patterns of thought, training, and habits developed over many years and after many other attempts to solve problems.

Some students quickly learn, from what the teacher stresses and what the teacher ignores, to study only the emphasized topics. These students succeed in getting very good grades in all tests, not because they know mathematics, but because they have correctly diagnosed the mannerisms of the teacher.

Stephen

When my nephew Stephen was small he asked his father to help him do an arithmetic problem. His father said, "Why don't you ask your uncle?"

Stephen replied, "I don't want to know that much."

When my nephew was in the third grade, I asked him if he liked arithmetic.

He answered, "I like arithmetic. This is a recording. I like arithmetic. This is a recording. I like arithmetic."

There are many unfortunate children to whom the beauty of mathematics will forever remain invisible.

What turns students on is important. But what turns them off is equally important.

Now

Part of the difficulty of education is that teachers are concerned with the future—our students are rooted in the now.

One-Third

On a visit to a fifth grade class I was changing fractions to decimals. We changed ½ to 0.5, ¾ to 0.75, and we even changed to ⅛ to 0.125. One of the girls raised her hand and said: "Yesterday, our teacher said that ⅓ equals 0.33333. . . forever and ever and ever. What does that mean?"

Well how was I to respond? Should I talk about infinite geometric series and the concept of a limit? I turned to the girl and said, "That's a very interesting question and a very important one. But it may take some time to explain it."

The little imp looked at me, grinned, and blurted out, "You don't know, do you?"

A Near Disaster

My first teaching experience was a near disaster. It took place at the Cleary school in Providence, Rhode Island while I was studying at Brown University.

The principal, when a teacher became ill, asked me to help out and teach a mathematics class. I started with the eighth grade on Monday. On Tuesday I was placed with the seventh grade class. By Friday I had worked my way down to grade four. Apparently, my willingness to help didn't match my ability to teach properly. It wasn't that I didn't know my stuff—I just didn't know the students I was stuffin'.

"Do You Love Mathematics?"

I had taught a mathematics lesson to some fifth grade students in a school in a large city.

Later, one of them in the class stopped me and asked, "Do you love mathematics?"

I paused for a long time and wondered: How do you answer such a question when it is asked—a question to which you have dedicated a lifetime?

~ Interlude ~
Best Friend

A dog is important because he is a bundle of love. A dog loves and makes no distinction of color, beliefs, nationality, or anything else that humans use as a criterion for friendship and affection.

- We will search for this kind of love in another human being for a whole lifetime and may or may not find it.
- We may search for this kind of love in our society and not find it.
- We may spend a whole lifetime trying to give the love which the little puppy has and shares with everyone.

Now tell me, wise one, if you were God, could you find a simpler way for a dumb animal to teach an important lesson to a wise man?

I've been associated with my basset hound for so long, that my friends don't make a distinction between us. They no longer ask me how I am, they feel my nose.

I had a basset hound, Rusty, who did not care particularly for Euclid's geometry and his straight line as the shortest distance between two points. When I took him out he walked as flies the butterfly.

I learned a great deal from my basset hound, Freckles: to be loyal and to turn around three times before lying down in bed. I was a softie where Freckles was concerned. Freckles would shiver and I would panic. He would nibble my fingers and I would think that he was in distress. I was all wrong in reading his signals.

As I teach now, I often pause and wonder if I am wrong also in reading some of my students' signals.

Chapter 7
Teacher's Impact

Our Impact

As teachers, we often frustrate our students by assigning tasks they cannot complete without ever giving them a chance to show off what they can do.

- We need teachers who have enough compassion to spot a little excellence in the midst of a lot of failure.
- We need teachers who care enough to point out a small achievement instead of dwelling on obvious shortcomings.
- We need teachers who give a gentle word of encouragement instead of thoughtless put-down.
- We need teachers who in the straight jacket of a cold professional vocabulary can introduce an extraordinary intimacy, gentleness, inspiration, and understanding.
- We need teachers who will bring to young minds the thrill and perpetual adventure of learning and who will keep youthful eyes alight with lasting wonder.

∽

Memory of a Child

As a teacher you can never predict what action you take or what words you speak that will be picked up and put away in the memory of a child—whether any will be among the unforgetable treasures of the classroom or among the things that memory would rather forget.

∽

And So Each Day

There are few teachers who have not experienced the warm welcome of an alumnus or an alumna who gratefully gushes over what we once said or did in class—and heaven help us, we cannot recall having said or done what the admirer admired us for.

And so each day I enter the classroom with a feeling of awe—realizing that my students will long remember me after they've forgotten even the subject that I taught them.

Perhaps this is, in the last analysis, what teachers are for.

Subjects change; time requires innovations; crises and technology implement changes faster; textbooks become obsolete; courses are dropped and new ones are added.

But amidst all change, the teachers are the only ones who come to class with perishable products wrapped in immortality, their own personality. The personality we teachers display will be reflected in the lives of students and transmitted by them to others in a chain that will end only when time is no more.

One cannot spend all the time with the useful—there must be time to look into the possibilities that the theoretical leads to.

One cannot spend all the time in discovery—after the discovery, there must be exploration and organization.

One cannot spend all the time in fun—there must be some academic responsibility and achievement.

The Little Things

Children do not understand or react to heroic gestures. They appreciate little things

- a smile,
- a nod of approval,
- an encouraging word.

Little things mean a lot to young boys and young girls.

A child's heart is in a child's hand. That is why a child, if the child loves you, will give you its hand so quickly and so often.

Teachers, you hold your students' hands for togetherness and often for safety, but you must let go for their growth.

Love in Many Places
We find love in many places

- in fiery autumn leaves,
- in crystal flakes frosted on window panes,

And most frequently we find love—in the love felt by the grasp of a tiny hand in ours.

Children and Sponges
Young children are like sponges.
They absorb all your strength, your energy, your vigor, your enthusiasm,
Leaving you listless, tired and limp as a sock—
But just pick up any one of them and squeeze tightly,
And somehow you get back all that you gave.

Now I know what I should have known when I first became a teacher—that students often aspire not to have the knowledge I share, but to be the kind of person I am.

Human Heart

The human heart cannot be bludgeoned into friendship and love,
You cannot buy enthusiasm,
You cannot buy loyalty or bribe the devotion of hearts and minds.
You have to earn and deserve these things.

Teachers know that words cannot open a student's heart. Only the heart of a teacher can open a student's heart.

Touches the Heart

What touches the heart? Cleverness?
No, this moves the mind.
What touches the heart?
Love and sympathy and understanding.

Teacher barks,
"For that Brenda, go to the board and write, 'I must not talk in class,' one hundred times."
Brenda writes,
"I must not talk in class 100 times."

Students will easily and quickly forgive a teacher for errors of the mind but hardly ever for errors of the heart.

Compliments

Teachers often receive compliments from their young students. But the one that ties their hearts into a knot is the little student with arms around the neck and whispering, "I want to be like you."

When They Accept . . .

I once asked a teacher, "How come students like you so much?"

She said simply, "I give them my heart and when they accept, they have to take the rest of me."

She was a teacher who heard her pupils with her ears, but understood them with her heart.

A little kindness and consideration among individuals is better than a vast love of all mankind.

What you do in the classroom each day is very important—because you are exchanging one day, each day of your life for it.

It is important that we educate one another with love and forbearance, each lending of his own strength to the weak, of his own knowledge to the ignorant, and of his love to all.

She was a teacher who taught students how to make a life rather than just a living, and her own life taught them to believe in her teaching.

Teacher:
Don't forget that little people can have big feelings.

Questions

I remember that in one class I used to ask the teacher a lot of questions. My teacher got mad at me, she thought I was an upstart.

You know, the teacher used to ask me a lot of questions but I didn't get mad at her.

In school I was a little frustrated and did not do too well. They asked me questions I could not answer. No one asked me questions about the talents I did have.

Many of us have been fortunate to have been touched by a teacher's magic, to have been uplifted in spite of ourselves, and to have been driven to exceed even our own dreams of accomplishment.

I once had a teacher who had many lines of experience etched around her eyes. Some people looked at her and saw there only the signs of age. Only a few recognized and read them as a mark of dedication.

My first day in kindergarten I was lonely and frightened. On the verge of tears, I was ready to run away from the classroom. And then the teacher came, bent down, and placed a kiss on my cheek that soaked into my heart. Strange—I was no longer lonely or afraid.

I have yet to be bored by those who praise me.

I Have Only Today

I know that my days with the young grow fewer each day.
I was tired and upset and impatient in class today.
But tomorrow all this I'll repay.
But time will not extend my stay,
And so I have not tomorrow
To be gentle and considerate and kind—
I have only today!

An infallible way to antagonize a student is to tell him simply, "You are wrong." Try it. It works every time.

A teacher should extend a student's curiosity, reward a student's performance, and continually stimulate her or his effort.

Be Always Gentle

A teacher learns very quickly that feelings can be found everywhere—in each word, in each casual look, in each act—and so a teacher learns to be always gentle.

Teachers should traffic in words and ideas, in feelings and hopes—and not just in groceries and hardware.

The understanding of another human being is an insight which can rarely be taught. Somehow, heaven knows how some acquire it, and others do not.

Loved and Adored

She was a third grade teacher. She was nothing spectacular although the third graders thought she was pretty and wonderful. As a matter of fact, she was a trifle homely, rather plain, and didn't seem to know how to match her clothes. The class loved and adored her. All because she was giving her best where there was no one to know or applaud.

As teachers we quickly learn that what is said in kindness is often more effective than what is said in truth to the students.

Teachers' hearts hold many shyly whispered secrets and confidences.

He charmed his students each day with his enchanting fantasy of universal childhood.

The Secret

The students adored their teacher because she spoke so enthusiastically and with concern. Some say that she spoke excellent English, but the secret was that she turned her speech into sorcery and cast a spell of love on all her classes.

Love is a many splendored thing and nowhere is it so openly visible, expressed, and practiced as in the classroom by devoted teachers.

Embrace Them

Teachers of young boys and young girls are like moms—they don't have age or color or size, and though they vanish forever in the eternal mists of time, memory has a way of keeping them forever alive in a grateful heart. Teachers who heed the needs of their students with their minds and embrace them with their hearts.

Teacher's Voice

The world needs teachers, who
Speak with a voice and
Respond with a heart, who
Make children forget a face and a body.
And children will then
Fashion a face and a body for the teachers whom they Will live
with and remember forever.

Fortunate the little girl and little boy whose teacher knows that it
takes time for a little girl and a little boy to grow.

Teachers and Peace

The greatest threat to humanity is not atomic missiles but human
indifference to humans. The only way to cure this indifference is
by education—by teachers who care for humanity.

And so peace for the future is in the eloquence and persuasive
power of teachers. Their concern is and has been for men and
women—today, tomorrow, and the forever future.

A teacher cannot urge scholarship without being a scholar.

Model

I am a teacher. By my words I am supposed to teach a subject, but
by my actions I am supposed to teach how to live a life. And so
often my students forget the words of my subject, but they never
forget the actions of my life. And so, why do I mark my students
on my subject when it is my life that they want to imitate? Why
does their transcript record how well they repeated the words of
my subject—rather than recording how well they imitated my life
of devotion, of sacrifice, and of scholarship? And so as a teacher, I
teach a subject but give inspiration for the imitation of a life.

∾ *Interlude* ∾
From the Institute

The following was given to me by a group of Summer Institute teachers when the Mathematics Institute at Boston College was housed in Devlin Hall.

> Our Father who art in Devlin
> Bezuszka be thy name,
> Thy students come, thy work be done
> In math as it is in physics.
> Give us this day a brief lecture
> And forgive us our questions
> As we forgive thou thine answers.
> Lead us not into contradictions
> But deliver us from rigor
> For thine is our future, our MASTERS, and our sanity.

Here is another poetic contribution from a staff member of the Mathematics Institute given to me during the Christmas season.

> On the first day of MATH 1-0-3
> My teacher gave to me
> One clear concept of infinity.
> On the second day of MATH 1-0-3
> My teacher gave to me
> Two short problems in number theory and one clear concept of infinity. . . .
> Three brief theorems from geometry,
>
> Four easy proofs using trigonometry,
> Five compact diagrams in graph theory,

Six tedious exercises on probability,
Seven lengthy tables of statistical accuracy,
Eight obvious algorithms for square rootery,
Nine precise rules for predicting eccentricity,
Ten clever tips on programmability,
Eleven trivial facts from mathematical history,
And twelve basic objectives for minimum competency.

Snoring and Clapping

Mike D. has been a friend of the Institute since its inception. He worked for NASA in its education program, and I often visited him at his office in the Ames Research Center at Moffett Field, California. On one occasion, he and I had a busy workday at a conference in Southern California where we were sharing a room. After a late supper we decided to get some sleep as the next day was to be equally demanding.

Mike was a rather large man and about a half hour after retiring, he began to snore. To halt his snoring, I got the bright idea of clapping my hands. Mike stopped snoring. But within twenty minutes he began to snore again, so I clapped my hands once more. Mike stopped snoring. However, in less than fifteen minutes he was snoring yet again.

At this point I got up and shook him saying, "Mike, for heaven's sake will you please sleep on your side or on your stomach. Your snoring sounds like the backfiring of a motorcycle."

Mike looked at me through sleepy eyes and said, "Stan, you should talk. Do you know what you do in your sleep? You clap your hands!"

Chapter 8
The Classroom

I've Grown Accustomed To . . .

Many a time, I have left the classroom saying to myself:

I've grown accustomed to this place—
I've grown accustomed to the young—
This is my place,
These are my people:
The small, the tall,
Those who are lost in wonder,
The few who seem to knowThe quick, the slow
The bright and those who only plod.
And on the slow, downhill drift of time,
These, these will forever be mine.

And if there is only one thing that you have to give to the young—
Let it be enthusiasm, kindled by curiosity, and guided by love.

In Class I Begin

In class I begin, "Now here is an important and interesting idea." And nobody pays attention.

In class I begin, "Here's one way of doing the problem." And some pay attention.

In class I begin, "This is on the test." And everybody pays attention.

The first day of class I asked my students, "Those of you who hate math stand up." No one stood up. I was pleased until I learned they were too lazy to stand up.

≈

Joey

I walked into the kindergarten.

I spotted him at once—

Joey with the ready smile and

The challenging eyes;

"Hi," I said.

"Hi."

"Can you tell me what two and two is?"

"Sure."

"What is it?"

"Five."

"But that's not right."

"You didn't ask me for the right answer."

He had me.

Do we confuse children with our *rights* and *wrongs*.

"O.K.," I said, "What is two and two? And I want the right answer."

"Why?"

I patted him on the head and walked out. Such encounters haunt the mind long after the words are gone.

Keep an eye on the Joeys!

≈

Different Answers

One of my beliefs is that it is far better to solve one problem ten different ways than to do ten problems using the same method.

One day in the fourth grade I stressed this belief after giving the students some problems to solve. At the end of the class, one little boy came to me with his paper and proudly said, "I did this problem in ten different ways."

As I was about to reward him with a pat on the head, he continued with, "And here are the ten different answers."

~

They Forget

In elementary schools, they forget over the summer what they learned the year before.

In high school, they forget what they learned a week ago.

In college, they forget what they learned yesterday.

~

I have never seen students with such wonderful memories—they can make the same mistake day after day.

~

In a mathematics class, I have learned never to ask, "Do you want me to go over that again?" Most students didn't want me to go over it the first time.

~

After my lecture on the differential in a calculus course—a lecture that was more than a little sticky and which overwhelmed the students—one student put up his hand and asked, "Are we responsible for the differential?"

A trifle upset, I answered, "No, thank goodness, Newton and Leibniz are."

~

I always remembered the end of each day in the first few grades of school—when the children with shy smiles waved at me with what was their whole hearts.

~

Proofs

Inference procedures and logical deductions are most difficult topics to teach. Many students often cannot develop a proof, usually do not see what you have proved, frequently do not know whether or not you have proved anything by a given proof, and incidentally could care less.

~

They say that at the end of the rainbow there is a pot of gold. In the classroom, there is always an end of a rainbow for any teacher that dares to chase it—and at the end of the rainbow there are the golden hearts of the young.

~

The Empty Classroom

The image of an empty classroom floods the night,
How could I have thought that without you—
Would or could there be any delight?

~

In all my classes, I sympathize with all those who walk the corridors of mathematics in darkness and live in the valley of the shadow of failure.

~

One lesson of the classroom that a teacher learns very early is: You can't push someone who is moving faster than you.

~

It has been well said, "Shouting in class to make students behave is like trying to steer a car by honking the horn."

~

Teachers? Who are they? Men and women who go to the classroom daily as to an earthly paradise.

~

Kingdom of Beggars

Teachers! We are a kingdom of beggars. Who else among people walks each day into a room full of children with love in their hearts and hoping that this love will be returned? Few parents thrill at the insight of a student as much as teachers. Few parents' hearts ache at the slowness of a student where gifts are lacking as much as the hearts of teachers.

~

Children in the kindergarten either screech like crows or speak in the musical tones of angels. It all depends on the state of your nerves.

~

The magic of the classroom each day is to see the unspoken love in the clear eyes of the young.

~

Students have a great power of passive resistance and indulgence. They let the teacher babble on.

~

Predictions

God made the weather in Boston. The meteorologists try to find out or guess what God is going to do next. Nowhere is there more opportunity to be wrong, except in the classroom with the very young, trying to predict what they will do or say next.

In the classroom the teachers are a love ever unfolding and giving, the students are a love ever accepting and nourishing.

Units and Dimensions

The teacher must emphasize the use of units and dimensions in applications of mathematics to the real world. Perhaps a humorous approach will help in the reinforcement of concepts:

- 2 pencils + 3 sharpeners = 5 pencil sharpeners.
- 2 floors + 3 walkers = 5 floor walkers.
- 2 barns + 5 dancers = 7 barn dancers.
- 4 dancers x 2 dancers = 8 square dancers.
- 2 pianos + 5 movers = 7 piano movers.
- 2 cows + 3 boys = 5 cowboys.

At the end of the class you summarize by saying, " I covered so and so and such and such."
Very good, but what did your students cover?

From personal experience with Lady Luck, I'm sure that there must be a law of probability that states that many things will happen contrary to probability.

Ignorance in the classroom is only when you don't know something and the teacher finds out.

Have you tried:
   The "W H" proof—Wave Hands proof
   The "W H W proof"—Wave Hands Wildly proof.

Love of the classroom is not an art that teachers acquire—it is their life.

Good Morning!

American education is really something. If you don't have a sense of humor you'll get ulcers. You know the way it is:

- You walk into the kindergarten or the first grade and you say, "Good morning." Everybody smiles and they wave their hands.
- You walk into a high school class and say, "Good morning." And everybody snarls at you.
- You walk into a college class and say, "Good morning." Someone looks quizzically at you and asks, "What do you mean by *good*?"
- You walk into a graduate class and say, "Good morning." And everybody writes it down!

Brown's Theorem

Bancroft Brown's geometry classes at Dartmouth College, in Hanover, NH, were always oversubscribed. He taught with insight, imagination, and humor. I remember some of Bancroft Brown's famous theorems:

- If two angles look equal, they are equal.
- Parallel lines never meet unless you bend one or both of them.
- If one angle of a triangle is 178 degrees, that doesn't leave a helluva lot for the other two angles.

Newton's first law of motion that "a body at rest will stay at rest unless acted upon by an outside force" is a law of physics—and also a law in a classroom that is conducted by a forceful teacher.

The most important things in a teacher's life are not things, but children.

Shy Smiles

I always remembered the end of each day in the first few grades of school—when the children with shy smiles waved at me with their whole hearts.

School classroom:

Where the real and ideal meet—but only once in awhile.

Butterflies

Why do butterflies sometimes land on your coat or even on your hand? Maybe so that you could wonder at the beauty and delicacy of this being, so wonderfully made.

In the same way, I wonder why of all people, I have been chosen to have these little children as my special care in the classroom, so delicate, so wonderfully made.

~ Interlude ~
Audience Appreciation

I once asked my sister how she liked my talk.

She replied, "You missed several wonderful opportunities to sit down."

I thought that I had gotten a standing ovation after my talk. Then I found out it was caused by someone jumping to his feet in an effort to beat the rest of the audience to the parking lot.

Some of my audience laugh at my stories only because they are afraid that if they don't, I'll tell the story again.

I told my sister a story. She said it wasn't funny. So I told it to a group at a meeting. They roared. So I said to my sister, "See."

She said, "They didn't mean it."

One way to stay awake during a banquet speech is to deliver it.

Many speakers begin their talk not knowing what they are going to say and ending it not knowing what they've said.

They say that my talks are not always good—but the digressions are delightful.

The frequent banquet speaker, besides having wisdom, humor, and eloquence should also have the digestive system of a goat.

Chapter 9
Motivation

Heart and Mind

I visited a fifth grade class recently. The students were most responsive to my numerical problems replete with puzzles and the discovery of number patterns based on what they had thought were the dull, routine addition and multiplication tables.

Later, one of the pupils in the class stopped me in the hallway and asked, "Do you love mathematics?"

I replied, "Of course I do".

The youngster paused and then continued, "Then please teach me the kind of mathematics that makes you love it."

Our conversation ended at this point because I had to rush off to visit another school. But I have not forgotten that child. He wasn't asking me to teach him the kind of mathematics that would guarantee him high marks and promotion; he didn't ask to be taught the mathematics essential for acceptance into college or graduate school. He simply wanted to have the kind of mathematics that he could love.

We have listened to educational gurus from all over the world: Piaget, Dienes, and others. We have written articles and books; we have filled our libraries with information on how a child learns. Yet, in our academic circles we do not have anyone who has told us how a child loves. Here is an idea that we mathematics teachers can pause over and think about. It is not the head that rules the child—it is the heart. Reach the heart of the child, and you will reach not only the child's mind but will in the process captivate the child's interest. Indeed, my young fifth grade friend with his youthful insight and conviction knew that whatever he would get to love, he would eventually master.

To attract aspiring mathematics teachers there must be, among other factors, a change in the content of the mathematics curriculum, in teaching strategies, and in motivational goals for the study of mathematics. Mathematics must be perceived as a joyful, meaningful, personal experience for students. If mathematics is everywhere around us, then mathematics should be for everyone. The teacher must reach all mathematics students and not just an elite few.

We face many challenges as we construct the mathematics curriculum of the future. How should the content be modified? What about the interface of technology and mathematics? What are the alternative courses to offer? There are so many variables to consider. But there is one constant:

> Once teachers and their students learn to love mathematics, they will love to learn mathematics.

A little girl of ten has her own wisdom and doubts and goals. A little boy of ten has his own hopes and fantasies and dreams. Mathematics becomes an unwelcome intrusion for them. As teachers we must carefully prepare our material with sensitivity and awareness of this very personal world of young people.

Some students with their first encounter with mathematics gain enough insecurity to last them a lifetime.

Textbooks, Manipulatives . . . Children
We get so concerned with textbooks, manipulatives, visuals, and curricula that we sometimes forget the real concern we should have—namely, our concern for children.

We forget that children are looking at this world with trust and innocence—and especially with big eyes wide open with wonder—and you have to show them Wonder-Full things to hold their attention and interest.

The day that wonder disappears from the world, will be the day when there are no more children in the world.

~

Curiosity

Curiosity is a wonderful and humiliating gift—because having curiosity is a spontaneous and eager confession of ignorance.

Hold on to curiosity!

If curiosity dies, life becomes like an eagle with a broken wing that has lost its ability to soar. Curiosity and imagination—two things that last a lifetime.

Two things that will outlast everyone's lifetime.

~

And Imagination

Children have an innate curiosity and a tremendous imagination. Because of this, children quickly get bored and lose interest in uninspired questions and dull details. The dullness of many classroom routines turns them off. We have to make the commonplace challenging and exciting.

~

Motivational Problems

Problems to motivate students in mathematics should

- have a dimension which evokes wonder and pleasure;
- give an insight into the mathematics which cannot be found by simply reading the textbook;
- produce interest and enthusiasm for the wonderful relationship between mathematics and the real world.

~

In the lamp of learning, curiosity is the wick, and when the wick dies out so does learning.

~

It has been well said that, "The cure for boredom is curiosity, and there is no cure for curiosity."

~

There are many paths to discover new ideas, new insights, new frontiers, but none is as powerful as curiosity.

~

The basic problem of all students is essentially the same:
- students need to have their curiosity stimulated,
- their interest aroused,
- and their enthusiasm kindled.

~

Listen to the rain beating on the school window panes:
Thirty-two problems, thirty-two problems, thirty-two boring problems.

~

Lots of Problems

There is no one set of general rules leading to the solution of all possible mathematical problems. How do you learn to solve problems? You keep solving problems, lots of problems, and keep acquiring different strategies. A universal algorithm that would solve all problems is a dream, an impossible dream.

~

Problems We Want

- Look for a dimension in a problem which evokes wonder and pleasure.
- Find problems that give an insight into mathematics that can not be found in even the clearest explanations.
- Find problems which produce a lasting interest and enthusiasm for quantitative relationships in and about the real world.

Basics of Motivation

The basics of motivation are:

- something interesting to do,
- something to love to do,
- something to look forward to doing.

There are teachers who can't wait to get up in the morning because they are fortunate to be inspired by the basics of motivation. When the day comes that you open your eyes in the morning and feel that there is no reason on earth for you to get up, then look around you very carefully—you may not be on earth!

What initiates mathematical discoveries? What initiates and nourishes creativity? Quite often it is, "Just suppose . . . " and "What if. . . ." Hardly ever do these two come from "If and only if. . . ."

Attitude and Love

A student's performance in mathematics is a product of yesterday's attention, interest, and perhaps some coercion from parents or sanctions from school administration—but attitude and LOVE of a subject will determine the student's achievement and future success.

Drudgery does not beget dislike. But dislike of a subject or a task will make every subject and task a drudgery.

Every teacher discovers sooner or later that much depends on the attitude of students rather than on their aptitude.

What is the real world interest for a child? Almost anything at the proper moment: a pebble, a friend, a flower, a little green worm, a math problem.

The mathematics that you learn with enjoyment you will not forget easily.

And so each day I pray:
   "Lord give me this day my daily idea."

Young students have many blisters and not enough calluses—the latter are just repeated blisters.

It could be that the greatest pleasure one can have is with one's own mind.

Calculators and Computers

What has been the impact of the hand-held calculator and the microcomputer as motivational elements for turning students on to mathematics and mathematics teaching as a career?

Some of the drudgery of computation has been eliminated, but elimination of this drudgery in and of itself has not motivated students to the love of mathematics.

Apparently, something more is needed than the elimination of computational drudgery, something more than the instant response, something more than a printed or vocal compliment from a flickering screen to change boredom into enthusiastic interest.

The millisecond miracles of the microcomputers are not enough enchantment to turn students on to the love and pursuit of mathematics. It will take motivated and motivating teachers to bring forth a generation of young enthusiastic mathematicians and mathematics teachers.

Our Raw Material

Students are the raw material of our schools and our task is to fashion a worthwhile product. The end product of our schools is always the student.

- In some cases we fail in our task.
- In some instances we get by.
- In some few cases, we are successful and this becomes our motivation and inspiration to continue in our task.
- And in some few instances we get benefits which we do not deserve, because the result is not of our inspiration or labor. The gifted, the talented, and the occasional brilliant happened to be in our classes and we were blessed with enough wisdom to stay out of their way.

Problem Solving

Problem solving is at the heart of mathematics, but we need problems with meaning, relevance, and motivation for:

- without motivation, there is no purpose;
- without purpose, there is no action;
- without action, there is no achievement, no progress;
- without progress, there is frustration, rebellion, and finally, neglect.

To look at the world with a child's wonder and search for answers with persistence. This has been the mark of genius.

Students in mathematics classes will discover that today's difficult mathematics problems will be their real life dilemmas tomorrow.

No matter how much experience we get, it will never be enough to live this life sensibly.

Problem solving in the schools is often considered a transition from the real to the unreal through the ideal.

Unravel the Unsolved

What a dreary and unimaginable world this would be if we only lived with solved problems. The beauty and challenge of life comes from our attempts to unravel unsolved problems. Even mankind's first paradise had a challenge!

Preparing

At present, a large population in our schools is no longer interested in finding answers to the meaning of life—only in preparing for a career. Making a living has priority over making a life.

Relevancy

Relevancy is a function of the times. It changes with the times. One cannot discuss relevancy in isolation. Relevancy is intimately related to the students' actual positions and their future potential in a society. Relevancy is also a function of the opportunities provided by a society.

For today's career and success-oriented students, the element of relevance is often quite different from that provided by academic core subjects. Quitting school and taking a dead-end unskilled job often seems more rewarding to a high school student than sitting through irrelevant classes with meaningless assignments.

~

Teach children that if they always work only for tomorrow, they will end up with a bunch of yesterdays.

~

One reason we teach is to have students be able to read the handwriting on the wall of their future.

~

In school, the teacher gives a lesson and then a test. In life, you get the test first and then the lesson, if you are clever enough to learn.

~

Charismatic Mathematics

Charisma, interpreted broadly, is a distinctive quality or special talent. It can be applied to objects and to people.

Charismatic mathematics is the special kind of mathematics that

- turns on the low achiever and the slow learner;
- turns on the reluctant learner and the underachiever;
- has something special for both the slow and the bright.

Charismatic mathematics is for the city and town, for the metropolis and the suburbs.

- It deals with the transitory and the eternal.
- It speaks the wisdom of the past in the language of the present.
- It weaves abstractions that clothe the real world in every age.

Now perhaps more than ever, we need charismatic teachers so that students will not succumb to terminal apathy.

~

Tell students to create eternal mathematics and very often they produce only ephemeral mathematics. But encourage students to produce only enough mathematics to be sufficient for the pleasure of the day, and some day they will create eternal mathematics.

One cannot motivate a love for mathematics by presenting mathematics as a succession of axioms, definitions, and theorems. This logical rigor leads to the rigor mortis of mathematics. Geometry was not invented or discovered by a succession of Euclids.

What I Learned in Mathematics

Some lines meet, some do not.
Some triangles are right, some are not.
Some numbers are whole, some are not.
Some fractions are proper, some are not.
Some numbers are rational, some are not.
Some decimals terminate, some do not.
Some decimals repeat, some do not.
Some numbers are real, some are not.
Some numbers are complex, some are not.
Some sets are countable, some are not.
Some workers are fast, some are not.
Some pools empty, some do not.
Some coins are true, some are not.
Some trains speed, some do not.
Some students like math, I do not!

Children and Butterflies

Have you ever watched children chase butterflies? The joy, the happiness, and the shouts of pleasure that come from their lips are due to one fact—the flight of the butterfly was whimsical, ever-changing, and unpredictable. This is why the elements of number patterns provide both motivation and pleasure—one never knows where the pursuit will lead and the pleasure and joy of new relationships, new discoveries are always there.

The path to these many enchanting hours may be a trifle difficult at times, but it is always full of mystery and fascination.

What we need in mathematics is—sight and insight—and then you might add one more—excite.

Motivating Students

Students come in various sizes, colors, and shapes.

They come from different environments, from different socio-economic levels. They come with different talents and abilities. Each one has personal hopes and ambitions.

For the teacher, the students are ever new and always different. But the task of the teacher has remained everlastingly the same—to encourage the disheartened, to move the slow, to guide the talented.

Success for the teacher has been complicated by a new problem. It is not a lack of talent and ability in the students. The problem is one of MOTIVATION—to motivate students to get involved in the work of the classroom.

Today, sheer content and well-phrased behavioral objectives are not sufficient. Today and for the foreseeable future, students will need motivation more than ever before—that sparks, that changes a disinterested and blank stare into a fire of enthusiasm.

This is a problem for all those in education: teachers, administrators, authors, and publishers. Our students live in a world of sound and color. To capture the attention of students in the classroom, teachers, and those who work with teachers, must compete with the professional results of the experts who produce the sounds and colors.

Students live in an expanding world of distracting entertainment. Therefore the subject matter of the classroom must be presented in a form interesting to students, effective enough to get a share of the students' time and their efforts.

Never more than now, the students are disenchanted by the lack of relevancy of many classroom activities. This lack of conviction in a task is far stronger a deterrent to learning than perhaps has been previously supposed. And so an important task for teachers, and those who support teachers, is that of motivation.

Motivation by sound and color—by content at appropriate levels which is appealing—by content that touches students in the real world in their own life styles and interests.

Mathematics Teacher of My Youth

I had a math teacher who for forty-four minutes each day had me on the edge of the chair in sheer expectation.

- She was tall, almost majestic.
- She was confident with an air of authority.
- She had the kind of smile and look about her that implied that she knew something wonderful and was just bursting to tell us.
- Each day I watched her as she waited outside the classroom door.
- But for her, it was not a classroom, she seemed to be peering into a full coliseum.
- The bell would ring, but for her it was the sound of rolling drums and trumpets.
- She seemed to smile a little, the slight acknowledgment to the cheers of the crowds.

- As she walked into the classroom, her heart beat faster, she paused, just long enough so that the master of ceremonies could proclaim,
- "And now, now I give you your teacher."
- She was there. It was time to begin!

I learned to love math—and I learned to love my teacher more.

Imagination and Logic

A child is born with an imagination whose potential is unlimited. But as the child grows older and older, this imagination is gradually stifled by exhortations to be sensible and destroyed by an immersion in logic.

I wonder why we boast of logic?

- As children, we don't have it.
- In youth, we disobey it.
- And in old age, it deserts us!

My fourth grade teacher spent a week teaching us subtraction. Then she spent another week teaching us subtraction by a different method. Then she said, "Forget about the other two methods. Now I'll teach you an easy way to do subtraction."

Why couldn't she have taught us the easy method at the beginning?

The Helpful Hand

Aaron was working on a problem. He was bogged down and obviously needed help. I interjected, "Aaron, want me to help you?"

He declined with, "I'd rather do it myself. I'll keep trying."

Help given too readily and too soon may often turn what is intended to be a favor into a future demand. There is a time to help a student and a time to be patient and just wait until the student comes and asks for help.

For What?

Students look upon mathematics as they do medicine. It is the evil smelling, the bad tasting medicine that is assumed to be good for them. The same opinion is held for the difficult, often boring, and always frustrating mathematics. It must be good for them, but the students ask, "For what?"

Enjoyment of the Mind

The emphasis and need now is for real world problems. But isn't enjoyment a real world problem? Are only shopping, unit pricing, interest rates, and investments real-world problems? Isn't the enjoyment of the mind a real world problem? Do you take a book and ask before reading it. "How does this solve my real-world money or job problems?" Can't we and don't we read just for enjoyment?

"When did you begin to like mathematics?" This question is rather trivial and has a simple answer. Children are born with a liking for numbers, for form, for patterns. The real question which we must find an answer to is, "When do children stop liking mathematics?"

There is nothing harder to understand than the obvious.

If the class gets bored, wake up the teacher.

What is "triumph" in a task well done? Well, it's just TRI-UMPH, a little umph added to a great deal of trying.

Smallest Motivation

Even the smallest motivation is worth more than

- ten threats,
- ten pressures,
- ten reminders.

Many a student gives the teacher the wrong answer because the teacher asked the wrong question.

Teach children to keep their youthful eyes alight forevermore with eternal wonder.

Never forget to introduce the intuitive and imaginative into mathematics.

The good teacher knows how to sort mathematical skills into

- the essentials,
- the desirables,
- the optionals and the luxuries.

Great teachers will always be theoretical motivational factors in a student's life.

Give us teachers whose goal it is to give students tasks and problems worthy of their human nature and not just menial assignments that a robot can do much more efficiently and speedily.

Challenge and Depth

Teachers make our world significant by the challenge of their questions and by the depth of their answers.

We should give very special lectures each day in class because our students are very special.

Teachers toil each day to spread ideas not only convincingly but also contagiously.

When asked how he came to invent relativity, Einstein replied, "By imaginatively challenging an axiom which others accepted uncritically."

Good teachers do this daily in the classroom.

Motivation is the moving element that prepares a child for loving. All that we call education, all that education will ever be in the future, was conceived in love.

Education has never been, nor will it ever be, only a spectator sport.

Sometimes I wonder if we are not taking mathematics along the road that made Latin and Greek dead languages.

Prepare for the opportunities of the big moments in the small moments.

Individualized Instruction

I heard someone say that individualized instruction consists in putting kids in closets on Monday and knocking on the door Friday to see if they are still there.

Each New Day

I have often tried to make my lectures resemble the waves breaking on the ocean shore. There is in each wave always something new, something different, something active, something crashing, something captivating, and also something quiet and peaceful that leaves a mark on the sands of the shore once the wave retires to the ocean—to begin again with another new wave.

With each new day, I try to be a new wave!

∿ *Interlude* ∿
Math Rhymes

An Assist from Elizabeth Barrett Browning

How do I love math?
Let me count the ways—
But nay, I could not do that
In an infinite number of days!

For years I studied numbers and such,
I now study calculus—
And still don't know much.

These two straight lines parallel be,
They never meet, you see.
Happy are they who believe because of an eye,
But more happy are they who believe in an unending sky.

∿

The Call à la Masefield

I must go down to the classroom again,
For the call of children is a clear call
That may not be denied.

∿

Metric Blues

Is one day as long as a meter?
Is a country mile exactly a liter?
Is grams the plural for grandpas and grandmas?   Or either?
I find the metrics clothed in mystery.
And my ignorance shows abysmally.
Is kilo a hundred? Or a million?
Is milli ten thousand? Or a billion?
Is deci just one part in a trillion?
I know some Latin, Greek, Hindustani, and even Swahili,
But the language of the metrics I don't understand, not really.
I always say mass when I mean weight—and vice versa.
Day by day it seems to get worser.
But with each blunder, hope grows intenser:
That if with utter confusion I now abound,
With equal stupidity I once did master the foot, the pint, and
the pound!

Chapter 10
Change

Resisting Change

There is a strong spirit of conservatism in us to keep unaltered all the old and familiar modes and patterns of living. This comes from an ancestral dread of all strange and new things. And it is difficult to break these patterns of instinctive resistance to change.

As young children, the intrusion of a stranger sends us scurrying for protection. As we grow older the change from home to the school becomes a traumatic experience for many. High school and college requires major adjustments and change. The search for a job after academic years includes its own challenges and fears.

But what about change in the educational arena amongst teachers, school committees, school administrators, and various school organizations?

The teaching profession also has an inherent disposition to resist change. The following is a humorous but incisive criticism of the way progress is inhibited in schools and of those who oppose blindly and irrationally all change.

Students today can't prepare bark to calculate their problems. They depend upon their slates which are more expensive. What will they do when the slate is dropped and it breaks? They will be unable to write.

Teachers' Conference, 1703

Students today depend upon paper too much. They don't know how to write on a slate without getting chalk dust all over themselves. They can't clean a slate properly. What will they do when they run out of paper?
Principals' Association, 1815

Students today depend too much upon ink. They don't know how to use a pen knife to sharpen a pencil. Pen and ink will never replace the pencil.
National Association of Teachers, 1907

Students today depend upon store bought ink. They don't know how to make their own. When they run out of ink they will be unable to write words or ciphers until their next trip to the settlement. This is a sad commentary on modern education.
The Rural American Teacher, 1929

Students depend upon these expensive fountain pens. They can no longer write with a straight pen and nib—not to mention sharpening their own quills. We parents must not allow them to wallow in such luxury to the detriment of learning how to cope in the real business world which is not so extravagant.
PTA Gazette, 1941

Ball-point pens will be the ruin of education in our country. Students use these devices and then throw them away. The American virtues of thrift and frugality are being discarded. Businesses and banks will never allow such expensive luxuries.
Federal Teachers, 1950

Today's students depend too much on hand-held calculators, micro-computers . . .
From Educators, not so long ago

The Three Stages of Change

The creative imagination that produces a feasible, viable idea.

The practical application and adaptation of the idea.

The diffusion of the idea through society and the acceptance of the idea by society.

As teachers, our objective in teaching is to change the world *and* to change *with* the world. Let the teachers lead and the leaders will follow.

What is one reaction to proposed changes? Those who cannot march to another's music often end up beating the drummer.

Very few can adjust to rapid innovations. Sudden and unexpected changes undermine a person's confidence and generate hostility.

Old Familiar Ways

There are some teachers who would rather not experiment with new modes of teaching, with new materials, or with new content. These teachers have become comfortable with the old familiar ways and find peace in changelessness. But the world does change, and teachers must change with the times.

A teacher's life is one of change. The teacher who walks the profession into a rut, deepens it into a grave. And the dulling sameness, the sure-footed comfort of the beaten path, is only for the beaten teacher.

The front edge of change is dangerously sharp. But that is where great teachers are found.

Phases

The educational system displays two phases. It passes from periods of no change to the panic of change at every moment.

Change is always helpful. It is needed most where a textbook, not mathematics, is taught.

Oldest, Newest

He teacheth best who loveth best,
The oldest and the newest,
For he knoweth that time doth change
The newest into the oldest.

Stability in All Change

I am sure that we all share the conviction that even in our most drastic transitions from one state to another, there have remained elements in the changes that were part of the heritage and tradition of humankind. And these elements were cherished, preserved, and transmitted with no change from generation to generation.

Thus, in spite of all change, be it slow or rapid, there is an underlying conviction among all people that:

- there is always a stratum of stability and permanency in all change;
- not everything changes, nor should everything change,
- not everything will change,
- all change must be balanced by the heritage and wisdom of a tried and accepted tradition.

Stages of Learning

The learning of the world passes through three stages:

- the wisdom of the ancients,
- the current stupidity,
- the return to the wisdom of the past.

Classrooms Frozen in Time

Now and then I have walked into
Classrooms frozen in time—
Classrooms in which there was no past, no future.
Classrooms in which there was only the present,
And the same thing was repeated day after day.

It was a strange classroom. It was a classroom where students spent happy days in yesterday, were uneasy to venture into the world of today, and were frightened of the world of tomorrow.

The Changeless Town

The town was small.
No change had occurred there for the last eighty years.
Nor would there be a change in the next fifty years.
The townspeople carefully buried their dead,
And carelessly buried their living.

To progress does not mean to travel a little faster along the same old roads.

It was a school where everything and everybody was in motion and yet going nowhere.

Shape Change

How can we as teachers meet the challenge to be relevant in this modern age? One thing is certain: organizations which do not serve their clients are doomed first to irrelevance and then to oblivion. Our task as teachers of mathematics is not only to adapt to change but also to help shape it.

Today, students and parents exert collective pressure in significantly affecting what subjects will be taught and what the content of the curriculum will be. Lack of student response has closed out courses and even whole departments.

Schools are now in a position very much like that of any business enterprise. They do not and cannot exist solely for themselves in academic isolation, but must serve the interests of the buyers. The seller, whether it be a supermarket, a department store, an elementary school, or a university, is becoming increasingly sensitive to the demands and sometimes to the whims of the purchaser. Education today is a buyer's market, and sellers must woo the public.

Some teachers, especially those with a love for and a professional interest in mathematics, may be disturbed by these commonplace analogies and comparisons. And that is understandable, for mathematics as a heritage of the human mind should be respected and revered by all.

To the Greeks, who synopsized centuries of unrecorded mathematical history in one word, *mathesis*, the root of the word, mathematics, meant knowledge. To want to know for the sake of knowing was to be human. Mathematics was a desire for a particular kind of knowing, a self-contained knowing based on autonomous thinking.

For a long time, this concept of mathematics cast a spell over men and women. Freedom and beauty, order and harmony, austerity and elegance—all these the soul of man forever seeks. In mathematics, there was some hope of attainment.

And so mathematics should not be compared to the market place of vulgar hawkers of corn and potatoes, of meat and grains.

For the traditional teacher, accustomed for years to a captive audience and convinced of the indispensability of mathematics in a truly humanistic core, the new trends are producing a traumatic experience. But regardless of the teacher's personal reaction, these are the facts of a real world which must be faced.

We have teachers ready to move from our safe and familiar ways to the challenge of all that is new and mostly unexpected.

Change begins with what happens in the classroom. It does not begin in the superintendent's office or the principal's office or in the curriculum committee.

We live in a world of change and change is one of our changeless certainties.

Mathematics has been compared to a tree which must grow each year into a new shape and bring forth a new fruitfulness.

Old Math, New Math, No Math

At one time there was the question of whether students would accept the New Math or the Old Math. Today, and for the foreseeable future, we have a greater question to answer, whether they will take any math at all.

For sheer survival, mathematics teachers must now look at their subject, not in academic isolation, but as a product in a competitive market attempting to attract students.

Mathematics must be properly displayed, attractively packaged, advertised, and presented to the prospective user with skillful persuasion.

The need for an imaginative curriculum and creative strategies of teaching is there—and so is the challenge.

No matter what mathematics we teach—the Old or the New—no matter how long we teach mathematics—it will always be difficult to teach people how to count their blessings.

Mathematics content and teaching methods must adapt not only to variations in ability but also to differences in emotional attitudes toward a subject that many have begun to dislike or fear.

A curriculum is very much like railroad tracks. You can't tell which way the train went by looking at the tracks. You can't tell what is happening in schools merely by looking at the curriculum.

A Constant?

I have taught mathematics for many years. Each year there are:

- v number of A's
- w number of B's
- x number of C's
- y number of D's
- z number of F's

The variation in the marks from year to year is very slight. The numbers remain practically the same. This result has been reported to me also by my colleagues.

Is this result a constant of our education? Can it be changed? How?

Is there a fatalism prevalent in our classrooms towards student mathematical achievement?

Is what turns a student to the love of mathematics more important than how a student learns mathematics?

Have we neglected the former and paid tribute in millions of dollars and hours to the latter? Should we continue this way?

They wrote a mathematics curriculum that was fifteen years before its time. It was ignored. Time passed. Fifteen years after its time, the mathematics curriculum was ridiculed. After a century, the mathematics curriculum was revived.

The curriculum we used in the first eight grades in my school didn't spiral—it just circled.

Two Types of Curricula

After looking at numerous mathematics curricula, I am convinced that there are only two types

- the obsolete
- the experimental.

It is regrettable that there are so many asking for something new, before they have time to examine and evaluate what is old and permanent.

Face the Problem

Several years ago, just as hand-held calculators were making their entrance into the schools, I mentioned in more than one talk with teachers:

"If tomorrow you walked into class and by some miracle your students could add, multiply, subtract, and divide, what mathematics would you teach them?"

The teachers smiled at me condescendingly. At that time it was almost unthinkable that this could happen. The question I proposed was an academic one of little impact or value on the lives of the teachers.

Well, today it is happening and in the future it will be more so. So we must face the problem now. How do you design a curriculum for students where computational skill is presumed and is no problem?

To survive the present revolution of science and technology, education, not wealth and weapons, is our best hope—the kind of education that gives largeness of vision which springs from contact with the best minds and treasures of our civilization.

Challenge of the Future

Computers remember, arrange, retrieve, and calculate. The lightning calculations of the computer are astounding.

We are living in a spectacular age of computers. The memory of a modern computer is practically unlimited. It can store and retain facts almost indefinitely. Compared to a computer, a human's memory is insignificant. Humans remember facts for about as long as a mirror reflects a face.

A long time ago, humans replaced the sweat of their brows by the steam of an engine. The machine freed people from some hard physical labor. It gave them time to rest and the leisure to think.

Today, humans have replaced the mental strain of memory by furrows on the brow of a magnetic tape. Humans have harnessed electrical power to do tedious arithmetical computations.

The computer has freed people from some mental labor, but not all of it. It has not freed humans from the most important part.

Humans can and must THINK! By this act, humans are superior. As long as humans continue to think, humans will outdistance the machine.

Catholics have a host of patron saints. Recently, we selected a patron saint for computers—he is St. John Damascene (pronounced damn machine).

The Wider the Frontiers

Due to the present information explosion, it is clear that no individual can read all the mathematical literature that is produced. Computers are used to extract important information from this mass of material. Yet even with the aid of the largest computers in the world, it is practically impossible for mathematicians to keep up with the developments in modern mathematics. Fortunately, much in mathematics is related. Information can be organized and categorized.

The information explosion in mathematics is indeed a challenge. One final thought:

"The wider the frontiers, the more opportunity there is for discovery."

It is quite possible that with technology, one machine may do the work of one hundred ordinary people. But it is still true, that no machine can do the work of one extraordinary individual.

There are many problems that must be addressed regarding the role of modern technology in the classroom. If we neither developed understanding nor taught problem solving well with paper and pencil algorithms, there is no assurance that we will be any better at it when computers and calculators are used to perform the operations we once did by hand.

Neither the hand-held calculator by itself nor the microcomputer by itself will instill mathematical understanding.

Effect the Changes

The time gap between major changes in technology, in economics, and in our social attitudes is getting shorter and shorter. Realizing that our own personal adjustment to change is still far too long, we must become change-oriented if for no other reason than that it is the only way to cope with the geometric explosion of change.

To discuss, plan, and effect the changes in mathematics, mathematicians, teachers, and administrators must cooperatively produce an educational content and strategy

- that does not neglect the nature of society,
- that is sensitive to the doubts, anxieties, and aspirations of students,
- that is professional in accord with the progress of mathematics,
- that is responsibly considerate of the constraints under which the teachers perform their daily tasks.

If any of these factors are neglected, then what is produced in a curriculum will be ill-balanced, irrelevant, or impossible to implement.

More Than a Textbook

Some mathematics textbooks are written in words withered by age and embalmed by repetititon. These books will not spread ideas contagiously. I have never met a mathematician who became great by just reading and doing exercises in a textbook.

In spite of our efforts in the schools, we sometimes produce trailblazers of mediocrity.

Procrastination

Procrastination grows

- it becomes a few hours,
- it becomes a day, a month, a year,
- it becomes too late.

The tragedy is that in this land where so many people can dream of being somebody and something, there now live people who don't want to be anything.

Reasoning requires preparation. You must observe, explore, and study things carefully before you begin reasoning about things.

Emphasize relations and order in your mathematics for they touch the uttermost reaches of time and space.

Our Age and Its Goals

About the glories of our age, historians have written that there has been

- no age so quick with invention,
- no age so able in healing,
- no age so rich in comfort,
- no age so exact in its science,
- no age so terrible in its wars,
- no age so commercial in its peace,
- no age so zealous in its education!

Let us grant all of that, but also add—there has been no age so ignorant and so confused about its goals!

This is a very blunt condemnation, but there is too much which is too valuable to lose in order that we pause and choose pretty words.

～

Problem of Applications

Today's standard problems in the applications of mathematics require revision and new techniques of teaching. There is hardly a teacher who will not agree that students have trouble with word problems. But that is not the complete truth.

- Students have trouble with the words, which frequently make no sense;
- they have trouble with the dimensions and units, which are seldom taught;
- they have trouble understanding the social and human implications involved in the problems, which are supposed to reflect real life and do not;
- they have trouble making the transition from dull, routine manipulations of numbers to word problems that often require the same manipulations.

～

Integrated with Life

Among the long list of behavioral and attitudinal objectives, the topics most frequently quoted today among educators that are essential to mathematics are

- some minimal competencies,
- pattern recognition,
- ability to generalize,
- skill to formulate imaginative solutions to problems that arise in, or describe, the real world.

In general, it is essential that mathematics be integrated with life, not mathematics as a preparation for life.

～

No plan, no strategy, no curriculum, no matter how ingenious, will ever influence education as long as these come from the minds of administrators and are not found in the hearts of the teachers.

Preparation

The users of mathematics can be found in practically every walk of life and in almost every subject in the academic curriculum. As a service science, mathematics must teach those concepts and those skills of computation that are useful for the homemaker, for the carpenter, for the storekeeper, in brief, for all the vocational personnel in our society.

At the same time, mathematics must be presented with sufficient depth and detail to be meaningful for the future physicist, chemist, engineer, and for all scientists who will be responsible for the development and advancement of our technology.

The makers of mathematics, namely, the mathematicians, look upon their subject as a discipline in its own right. Mathematics must attract its share of students who will pursue the subject with the same interest and dedication as the physicists, chemists, geologists, and biologists do their own specialties.

Solid preparation for a career in an enormously expanding subject such as mathematics must begin as early as possible.

Start Earlier

There is a story of the commuter who ran to catch his train. On missing it, he said, "If I had run faster, I would have made it."

A bystander replied, "No, if you had started sooner, you would have made it."

You cannot make up education by running faster. You have to start earlier.

Not the Same

It is quite obvious that we cannot give different children the same subject matter for the same length of time and expect the same degree of mastery. However, it is possible to vary the content and/or the time element. Thus, units of content must be determined, the degree of mastery specified, and the amount of time to each unit allotted.

We cannot, as teachers, be complacent to remain in the status quo—that's Latin for the mess we're in.

We need higher academic standards in our schools. However, the quest for higher academic standards in schools carries all the connotations of the search for the Holy Grail. Today, many think that the quest is further away than ever.

Searching for Answers

There are three great questions to which people are always searching for answers. Questions that must be answered either by our own efforts or with the help of others.

- Is it right or wrong?
- Is it true or false?
- Is it beautiful or ugly?

Our education ought to help us to answer these questions.

An effective teacher training program should prepare men and women to create the new ideas of tomorrow and not produce technicians for the embalming of the concepts of yesterday.

144

Knew All the Answers

I sometimes wonder why my supervisors did not expose me to all the problems of curriculum changes, class management, and so on when I was twenty-five and knew all the answers.

Mathematics isn't what it ought to be. Mathematics isn't what it's going to be. And one thing is sure—mathematics will never be what it was.

We have been discussing educational changes for the future, how to meet the problems and challenges that will arise. But, looking at the way the world now appears to be going, maybe, our only problem for the future is to make sure the human race does have a future.

Little Me!

Not long ago, wanting to impress upon her young students in the fourth grade the recent rapidity of change and the wonders of our technological development—the radio, the television, the jet plane, and space rockets and shuttles—a teacher asked, "Can anyone tell me, what is here today that was not here fifteen years ago?"

A little girl waved her hand excitedly, stood up and said, "ME!"

She was not only right, but with youthful insight pinpointed our tasks as educators—the greatest change occurs in our classrooms year in and year out when all the little MEs come to us. In our fast-changing age they must somehow be prepared for tasks and jobs that as yet do not exist, and they must be counseled and directed to bypass skills that will be obsolete when they are ready to enter the workplace.

Logically Speaking I

Notice from the US Department of Education:
"Are you illiterate? Write today for free help."

~

Notice in US Navy Bulletin:
"Classified material is considered lost when it is not found."

~

Surgeon General of USA:
"With smoke pollution the way it is, even if we were immortal we would all die of cancer."

~

US senator in congressional speech:
"I deny the allegation and the alligator."

~

US senator to reporter:
"No comment and that's off the record."

~

Letter to the editor of a newspaper:
"Since crime is the number one problem of our country, we should make the death penalty more severe."

Chapter 11
Reflections

Reading, Writing, 'Rithmetic

Once upon a time, the elders of a town got together and they said, "We must get a teacher to teach our young ones."

"What must the teacher teach them?" said the elders.

An old patriarch rose and said, "Reading, the teacher must teach them reading—reading minds and hearts. The teacher must have this gift. The teacher will have to read the minds and hearts of our young children and then teach them how to read the hearts and minds of other men and women. For this is the curse of our age. We have so many who can read papers and books, but so few who can read the minds and hearts of men and women—their weaknesses, their temptations, their hopes, their aspirations. We need men and women who can read these and understand."

"What else will the teacher teach them, old one?" questioned the elder.

"Teach them writing!" thundered back the old patriarch. "Writing by the deeds of men and women! Not writing in words bound by books which lie dead in the dank storage of libraries, but writings in the work of men and women who leave their words and actions as blisters on the lips of living people. Teach them to write by deeds, by uprightness, by the power of truth, by the needs and passions and honor and dedication to obligation. The teacher must teach them to write these so that all who pass by will stop and read and never forget."

"And is there anything else, old one, that the teacher must teach them?"

"Yes," replied the patriarch, "the teacher must teach them 'rithmetic; teach them to count the folly of pride and prejudice; teach them to number the abuses of power and to number those who fell to the folly of prejudice; teach them to number the good and to subtract the weak, to multiply the strong, and to divide those who fail. The teacher will do 'rithmetic caring for the straggling one rather than the safe ninety-nine."

The elders listened to the old patriarch and some agreed.

But then rose the young leader who spoke of the same needs, but in the spirit of the needs of the time. The leader agreed that the young ones needed reading—but reading to know which sides to take, to know who is who and what is what, and to learn how to be persuasive.

The elders nodded in approval, for this was life.

Oh, the young leader agreed that the children must learn to write, but to hedge the truth with a path of escape, to write so that people would find it hard to understand and harder still to make a case before a court.

And the young leader agreed that the children should know 'rithmetic. The hard common sense of dollars and cents, for this is what counted in life.

Then the young leader turned to the old patriarch and exploded, "Old one, your days are over! You live in the past, somehow you have preserved enough acumen to remember that reading, writing, and 'rithmetic are important—but not yours—ours!"

The elders deliberated as to which teacher to pick. And they did pick one—the old patriarch's or the young leader's? Their choice will always be their curse or their salvation!

∼

The Present—The Future
To mold the present, we have only the lessons of the past—and it is this present that we must use to determine the future.

∼

Understanding

There is nothing in the world more important than understanding

- understanding the world we live in,
- understanding the people we live with,
- understanding ourselves,
- understanding our ambitions and our goals,
- understanding our values!

And to acquire all of these we need teachers, teachers with vision and insight.

How many of us fall into the category:

Mathematician—a remote, lonely, abstract thinker of useless thoughts who can be lovable and infinitely good-humored.

Happy Because of Mathematics

I'm glad there is mathematics!

I'm happy that no one can find a largest number—a grade school child can always add one to the number and win.

I'm happy that no one can find the smallest number—the child can always take one-tenth of the number and have a smaller number.

There is an element of satisfaction in mathematics. It takes the smugness out of the proud and stings the tyrant.

No matter what the smug and the tyrant can achieve—these two tasks they cannot accomplish and a child can show that they cannot be done.

What Are We Talking About?

Bertrand Russell has defined mathematics as the science in which we never know what we are talking about or whether what we are saying is true.

Now mathematics has been shown to apply widely to many other, if not most, soft and hard sciences.

It follows therefore, that most other scientists do not know what they are talking about or whether what they are saying is true.

We often say that mathematics is an art and a science. Unfortunately, we frequently teach only the science. Art is humor and enjoyment, it is life and caricature. Art is beauty and the sudden discovery of a hidden wonder. You know it may be only in the art of mathematics that some of our students will gain recognition rather than in the science of mathematics.

You cannot wrap memories around your cold shoulders and expect to feel the warmth of a human arm.

Just when I get to the point where I begin to envy the children and their youth, I get cured at once by looking at a student carrying an Algebra 1 book.

You remain young when you are around the young—you get old when you try to keep up with them.

The thing that worries me most about the young student generation is the fact that I no longer belong to it.

Baseball Fractions

It happened in my fifth grade. The teacher put

$$\frac{1}{2} + \frac{1}{3} =$$

on the chalkboard and asked for volunteers to do the sum. I raised my hand and the teacher sent me to the board. I wrote

$$\frac{2}{5}$$

quickly and firmly on the board.

The teacher looked at the answer and said, "That's wrong!"

I was just impertinent enough to ask, "Why?"

The teacher looked at me with open impatience and said, "No one adds fractions that way!"

I didn't quite understand her logic, I had just added the fractions, "that way."

What my teacher didn't know about little boys would have filled a large book.

Each evening after supper, my friends and I would walk to the city square, to the local newspaper office to study the results of the day's baseball games which were printed on a large bulletin board. This was the era of the great Yankee baseball team with players, Babe Ruth, Lou Gehrig, Tony Lazzaro, and a host of other baseball greats.

This particular day, the Yankees played a double header. Babe Ruth had one hit out of two times at bat in the first game and one hit out of three times at bat in the second game. My friends and I computed quickly Ruth's batting average,

$$\frac{1}{2} + \frac{1}{3} = \frac{2}{5}$$

two hits out of five times at bat. Ruth had batted .400 that day.

We did this kind of computation with fractions day in and day out during the baseball season from April through September and into the World Series. Yet there was my teacher telling me that no one adds fractions, "that way."

Later on, at the summer twilight baseball games, I found out that the newspaper reporters also added fractions, "that way."

Only the butcher, the baker, and the candlestick maker added fractions the way my teacher did, but apparently not her little trouble maker.

$\sim$

More on Baseball Fractions

In recent years, during my visits to the classroom, I have baited students with my baseball fractions story of

$$1/_2 + 1/_3 = 2/_5.$$

The reaction to the addition method has not been uniform. There were two incidences that I remember clearly. In a school in Texas, I asked some fifth graders to add,

$$1/_2 + 1/_3 =$$

There were groans and sighs. Finally, someone said,

$$5/_6.$$

I asked the student, "How did you get the answer?"

There followed the student's long explanation of common denominators, least common denominators, and so on and so on. Then I went to the board and wrote,

$$2/_5.$$

The student looked at the answer and said that it was wrong.

I urged, "But isn't my way easier than yours?"

The student admitted that the method was easier but it was not right. I persisted with, "Just a moment, who decides what is right or wrong in mathematics?"

The student answered, "Mathematicians."

I countered with, "Well, I'm a mathematician!"

The student rebutted, "No you're not, you're a preacher!"

Later in a school in Michigan, I came to the climatic line, "Well, I'm a mathematician."

At which point the student won with the remark, "I'm a mathematician too, so what?"

In every school, I have tried to explain and promote my baseball fractions, but I was a leader with no followers.

Five and One-Half Workers

I continued to have problems with fractions. In junior high one day my teacher gave us a story problem that called for finding the number of workers needed to dig a hole subject to certain conditions.

I worked like a little beaver to solve the problem. I raised my hand and gave an answer: "five and one-half workers."

My teacher laughed at me and so did the class. Exasperated, I blurted out, "Look, I didn't make up the problem, I only solved it."

I was furious—a fraction answer was reasonable—newspapers reported statistics that said the average American family had two and one-half children and the like. If my teacher was preparing us for the real world, it certainly was not on this planet.

Our Time

When our time in the past is so much longer than what is left for our future—we either redouble our efforts or quietly and peacefully resign from all turmoil and strife.

Nostalgia:
Recalling with happiness those first few years of teaching about which we weren't so crazy then.

You have young children in your class and pffft—they're old.

As time goes on, one hopes to see fire in the eyes of the young and light in the eyes of the old.

Forever is not really a long time, it gets shorter day by day.

There is no sunset in teaching, there is only perpetual dawn.

Resolve to be tender with the young, compassionate with the aged, sympathetic with the striving, and tolerant with the weak and the wrong. Because in your life, you will have been them all.

A Teacher No Longer

They told me today—I was through.

Fifty years it was—one hundred times that many students.

Years of chalk dust, years of young faces:

> looking,
> searching,
> mostly yearning, for the
> secret that supposedly we held, that would:
> explain all,
> clarify all,
> simplify all.

Yet not once did I say

> anything else but—the eternal search is ours too, not just theirs;
> that if ever found, it will be each one's, not the crowd's.

Now a younger teacher will meet them,

And there will be chalk dust and young faces:

> looking,
> searching,
> yearning, for the secret.

And the young teacher will grow old

In the search, just as we did,

But perhaps there is no secret,

And the mystery dissipates in knowing one's self,

Not in knowing the heavens, the seas, and the earth.

> Would that I
> Had spent more time on that
> Rather than on the heavens, the seas, and the earth.

I'm at the age now where everything I say reminds me of something else.

When I was young I was taught to respect my elders. Today, I'm at the stage where I don't have anybody to respect.

~

To My Students

What will I do when my days with you are through?

When each morning no longer holds an imperative to rise and be with you?

I know that memory will wake me and I will spend the days recalling all the times I shared with you.

~

Growing Old

The effects of growing old hurt most in the heart. The hurt comes when one has to give up doing the things one did and would like to continue doing—but cannot.

For Whatever Days Be Left

This I desire for whatever days be left for me:

A mind clear and true to guide those who look to me,

Eyes to see the good in children that others miss or do not see,

Hands to touch and heal the many sorrows of the young each day,

Lips that smile a contagious happiness and friendship,

The patience of a gardener, who does not seek to reap overnight, and

A heart that gladdens other hearts, and only brings them sorrow when I am no more.

～ *Interlude* ～
Logically Speaking II

Statistical reasoning is uncertainty reasoning. In an office of an insurance company there were fifty men and two women. A report on the marital status of the office had:

> "Two percent of the men in the office are married to fifty percent of the women."

～

Mother to child:
"Now dear, eat both sides of your bread."

～

Man to his wife in an art gallery:

> "Dear, don't stop to look at anything, because that way you won't see anything."

～

To parting guest:

> "Come see us again soon—we miss you almost as much as if you were here."

～

Casey Stengel:

> "Line up alphabetically by height."

～

Notice in church bulletin:
"The south and north ends of the church will be used this afternoon for baptisms. Children will be baptized at both ends."

~

Notice to customers:
"All telephone inquiries must be in writing."

~

Sign in a loan office:
"Now you can borrow enough to get completely out of debt."

~

Sign in store window:
"Any faulty merchandise will be cheerfully replaced with goods of the same quality."

~

Sign at airport:
"The takeoff distance shall not be greater than the length of the runway."

~

Famous newscaster:
"If there is a 50-50 chance that something can go wrong, then 9 out of 10 times it will."

~

Famous physicist:
"Prediction is very difficult—especially about the future."

~

Famous mathematician:
"If you put infinitely many things in a small space, some of them will be pretty close together."

Chapter 12
Poking Fun at Bureaucracy

Who Has All the Answers?

Archimedes, the great Greek mathematician, scientist, and inventive physicist, was soaking in a public bath when the principle of specific gravity became clear to him. He was so excited that he leaped from the bath and ran home naked shouting: "Eureka!" (I've found it!)

Suppose now that school personnel and/or students were Archimedes. How would they have behaved in his situation?

Suppose Archimedes was the:

Superintendent:
> Discovers the solution to the problem, dresses, cleans the tub, then walks dressed up into the street and whispers: "Eureka."

School Board Member:
> Discovers the solution to the problem and puts it aside for the next board meeting.

Principal:
> Takes time to grab a towel, then rushes into the street shouting: "Guess what? Eureka!"

Vice-Principal:
> Discovers the solution to the problem but forgets to tell anyone.

Chairperson of the Department:

Is in the tub and on the verge of the discovery of the solution to the problem when interrupted by a family member who wants to use the bathroom.

Assistant Chairperson:

Gets into the tub while thinking of the problem, but has poured too much water in the tub which now overflows, and spends the rest of the time cleaning up.

Senior student:

Takes a bath, but spends time playing with the rubber duck and boat—never solves the problem.

Junior student:

Takes a quick bath because there's no hot water and the water is too cold to think of the solution to any problem.

Sophomore student:

Takes a shower instead of a bath and so misses the opportunity to discover the solution to the problem.

Freshman student:

Forgets or hardly ever takes a bath—never makes a discovery of the problem.

You Asked

Remember? You asked in high school, "What good it this?"

"You'll find out in college," they answered.

In college you asked, "What good is this?"

The response was "Didn't they tell you in high school? No, well then, go back and ask."

You can tell the incompetence of a school organization by the number of its committees.

Most school committees meet in rooms where the conference tables are round—it facilitates passing the buck.

≈

Meetings
In a school system, a problem often requires several meetings for a solution. But if the number of meetings increases, the meetings become more important than the solution to the problem.

≈

School board member:
"We must teach Latin. It's the only dead language that will live forever."

≈

Schools and Their Troubles
The trouble with some of our schools was diagnosed as follows:
- teachers are afraid of the principal;
- the principal is afraid of the superintendent;
- the superintendent is afraid of the school board;
- the school board is afraid of the parents;
- the parents are afraid of their children;
- and the children are afraid of nobody.

≈

School fire drill instruction:
"Teachers must close the door before they leave the classroom."

≈

Senator on education commission:
"Children are very poor today in arithmetic. They can't divide six by one-half and get three."

≈

Laugh or Cry

I was asked, "How can you be lighthearted and humorous about the sorry state of our school system?"

"Because," I replied, "if I didn't laugh, I'd have to cry."

Teacher:
"You received a forty on your test."

Student:
"What do you mean a forty on my test?"

Teacher:
"Oh, I'm sorry—which of my words don't you understand?"

A local high school has put up a sign:
"Beware of students going to and from school."

A good warning, especially if the students are driving a car.

Another school sign read:
"Drive carefully. Don't hit our students."

Message scribbled below:
"Try for our teachers."

Principal to teacher:
"You're a very good teacher. However, by your hard work, efficiency, promptness, loyalty, and friendliness, you're setting a bad example for the rest of the teachers."

Delegate—Appropriate

The successful superintendent has the sense to delegate all responsibility, the instinct to shift all the blame, and the ability to appropriate all credit.

A superintendent is like the bottom half of a double boiler. This person lets off a lot of steam but really doesn't know what's cooking.

When you strongly believe and love something, go after it yourself—don't form a committee to distract you.

Principal's memo:
   "I've repeated to you a million times! Cut out all needless duplications!"

Overheard at a principals' meeting:
   "It's difficult to soar with eagles when you work with turkeys."

Principal's prayer:
Lord, please make all the bad teachers good, and all the good teachers easier to deal with.

Final Thoughts

Lasting Dreams

There will always be dreams for me.

For I dream of the ones I teach and guide—

A class of future laborers, government and commercial
personnel, scientists, mathematicians, scholars, teachers—

Each one a dream

To be guided and nourished—

To be loved, scolded, cherished, held close,

And then let go—

Like dreams that disappear with the dawn.

But resurgent miracle—

It happens that the dreams

Reappear with each new school year—

And so, there will always be dreams for me—

As long as there are

The young to people them.

∽

A Teacher for All Seasons

Spring:
    start a child in the adventure of learning.

Summer:
    see the full bloom of the child-man and child-woman.

Autumn:
    ensure the fullness of a child's hopes and dreams.

Winter:
    provide for those days of rest replete with memories of a life
    crowned with fulfillment.

~

The Gift of Love

I told them that I loved mathematics!

They scoffed and challenged me:

    To stop the daybreak with my quadratics,
    To make the day longer or shorter with relativity equations,
    To find the number that can measure human ills,
    To mend a heart or dry a tear with a plus or minus sign!

I left them and wondered:

    Was my dedication in vain,
    When what people valued most was not in my realm?

I left them and wondered:

    Should I turn my efforts to harness the flight of the rising
    sun?
    To shorten minutes of pain and lengthen hours of joy?
    To delay until the day after forever the onset of a shattered dream?
    To hasten the end of a day with memories wishfully to be
    forgotten?

But then as I wondered:

I remembered that someone else rules the speed of daybreak,
Who makes the day and measures the flight of night,
Who knows the number of human ills,
Who in His own way and time inspires new dreams and
transforms memories.

But most of all I knew:

That He gives to me the gift of love—
To continue in what I want to do best—
To be a teacher!

Glorious Heritage

Mathematics makers and mathematics teachers are an important
part of our civilization. They have left us a lasting heritage of the
mind and heart. It is a heritage that was born of the freedom of the
human mind—a mind free to question, free to think, and free to
wonder and explore all the What Ifs? This heritage is also a brilliant
and unending quest for the practical and the apparently useless, a
paradoxical combination of reality and dreams.

The heritage of mathematics continues in today's teachers—for we
in the present are an echo of yesterday and the voice of tomorrow.
From the wisdom of the past, we know that very little that is
important is ever achieved without dreams. From the needs of the
ever present hour, we have a task to shape our present into harmony
with our aspirations.

And when will this glorious heritage end? This is the enduring
spell, at once prophecy and history of the heritage we affirm. With
your help, it will never end.